SACRAMENTS IN SCRIPTURE

SALVATION HISTORY MADE PRESENT

*To Father Richard Rohrer,
whose love of the liturgical and
sacramental life of the Church has been
a true blessing to me, my family,
and so many people.*

SACRAMENTS IN SCRIPTURE

SALVATION HISTORY MADE PRESENT

TIM GRAY
FOREWORD BY SCOTT HAHN

EMMAUS ROAD PUBLISHING
Steubenville, Ohio

Emmaus Road Publishing
1468 Parkview Circle
Steubenville, Ohio 43952

Library of Congress Control Number: 2001088762
ISBN: 0-931018-04-9
ISBN: 978-1-931018-04-3

Unless otherwise indicated, Scripture quotations are taken
from the Revised Standard Version, Catholic Edition (RSVCE)
© 1965, 1966 by the Division of Christian Education of the
National Council of the Churches of Christ in the
United States of America. Used by permission

Excerpts from the English translation of the
Catechism of the Catholic Church for the United States of America
© 1994, United States Catholic Conference, Inc.—Libreria Editrice Vaticana.
English translation of the *Catechism of the Catholic Church:
Modifications from the Editio Typica* © 1997,
United States Catholic Conference, Inc.
—Libreria Editrice Vaticana.
Used with permission. Cited in text as "Catechism"

Cover design by Mairead Cameron
Layout by Beth Hart

Nihil Obstat: Rev. James Dunfee, *Censor Librorum*
Imprimatur: ✠ Most Rev. Gilbert I. Sheldon, D.D., D.Min.
Date: September 26, 2001

The *Nihil Obstat* and *Imprimatur* are official declarations
that a book or pamphlet is free of doctrinal or moral error.
No implication is contained therein that those who have
granted the *Nihil Obstat* and *Imprimatur* agree with
the contents, opinions, or statements expressed.

CONTENTS

ABBREVIATIONS

Old Testament
Gen./Genesis
Ex./Exodus
Lev./Leviticus
Num./Numbers
Deut./Deuteronomy
Josh./Joshua
Judg./Judges
Ruth/Ruth
1 Sam./1 Samuel
2 Sam./2 Samuel
1 Kings/1 Kings
2 Kings/2 Kings
1 Chron./1 Chronicles
2 Chron./2 Chronicles
Ezra/Ezra
Neh./Nehemiah
Tob./Tobit
Jud./Judith
Esther/Esther
Job/Job
Ps./Psalms
Prov./Proverbs
Eccles./Ecclesiastes
Song/Song of Solomon
Wis./Wisdom
Sir./Sirach (Ecclesiasticus)
Is./Isaiah
Jer./Jeremiah
Lam./Lamentations
Bar./Baruch
Ezek./Ezekiel

Dan./Daniel
Hos./Hosea
Joel/Joel
Amos/Amos
Obad./Obadiah
Jon./Jonah
Mic./Micah
Nahum/Nahum
Hab./Habakkuk
Zeph./Zephaniah
Hag./Haggai
Zech./Zechariah
Mal./Malachi
1 Mac./1 Maccabees
2 Mac./2 Maccabees

New Testament
Mt./Matthew
Mk./Mark
Lk./Luke
Jn./John
Acts/Acts of the Apostles
Rom./Romans
1 Cor./1 Corinthians
2 Cor./2 Corinthians
Gal./Galatians
Eph./Ephesians
Phil./Philippians
Col./Colossians
1 Thess./1 Thessalonians
2 Thess./2 Thessalonians
1 Tim./1 Timothy

2 Tim./2 Timothy
Tit./Titus
Philem./Philemon
Heb./Hebrews
Jas./James
1 Pet./1 Peter
2 Pet./2 Peter
1 Jn./1 John
2 Jn./2 John
3 Jn./3 John
Jude/Jude
Rev./Revelation (Apocalypse)

Documents of Vatican II

SC   Constitution on the Sacred Liturgy
(*Sacrosanctum Concilium*), December 4, 1963

IM   Decree on the Means of Social Communication
(*Inter Mirifica*), December 4, 1963

LG   Dogmatic Constitution on the Church
(*Lumen Gentium*), November 21, 1964

OE   Decree on the Catholic Eastern Churches
(*Orientalium Ecclesiarum*), November 21, 1964

UR   Decree on Ecumenism
(*Unitatis Redintegratio*), November 21, 1964

CD   Decree on the Pastoral Office of Bishops in the Church
(*Christus Dominus*), October 28, 1965

PC   Decree on the Up-to-Date Renewal of Religious Life
(*Perfectae Caritatis*), October 28, 1965

OT   Decree on the Training of Priests
(*Optatam Totius*), October 28, 1965

GE   Declaration on Christian Education
(*Gravissimum Educationis*), October 28, 1965

NA   Declaration on the Relation of the Church to Non-
Christian Religions (*Nostra Aetate*), October 28, 1965

DV	Dogmatic Constitution on Divine Revelation (*Dei Verbum*), November 18, 1965
AA	Decree on the Apostolate of Lay People (*Apostolicam Actuositatem*), November 18, 1965
DH	Declaration on Religious Liberty (*Dignitatis Humanae*), December 7, 1965
AG	Decree on the Church's Missionary Activity (*Ad Gentes Divinitus*), December 7, 1965
PO	Decree on the Ministry and Life of Priests (*Presbyterorum Ordinis*), December 7, 1965
GS	Pastoral Constitution on the Church in the Modern World (*Gaudium et Spes*), December 7, 1965

*All quotations from the documents of the Second Vatican Council are taken from Austin Flannery, O.P., ed., *Vatican II: The Conciliar and Post Conciliar Documents*, Northport, NY: Costello Publishing Co., copyright © 1975.

General Directory for Catechesis

Throughout the text, the *General Directory for Catechesis*, published by the Congregation for the Clergy and approved by Pope John Paul II on August 11, 1997, will be cited as "GDC."

FOREWORD

The sacraments are what God had in mind for you and me "in the beginning," when He made the heavens and the earth. The sacraments are what He brought about, little by little, all through the Old and New Testaments.

This may come as a surprise to many readers. Though we Catholics love and revere the sacraments, too often we treat them as something the Church teased out of a smattering of New Testament proof-texts. That notion, however, is precisely backwards. It would be more accurate to say that the Bible is what God's people teased out of a providential plan in which God's New Covenant sacraments were already present "in mystery" (to steal a phrase from the Church Fathers) from the first moments of the Old Covenant.

There is a unity to the two Testaments of the Bible; and the whole of the Bible is inseparably united with the small details of the Church's life today.

Jesus Himself read the Old Testament this way. He referred to Jonah (Mt. 12:39), Solomon (Mt. 12:42), the Temple (Jn. 2:19), and the brazen serpent (Jn. 3:14) as signs pointing to His own life, death, and Resurrection. Toward the end of Luke's Gospel, Jesus took "Moses and all the prophets" and "interpreted to [His disciples] in all the scriptures the things concerning himself" (Lk. 24:27). Saint Paul followed His Master in this reading of the Hebrew Scriptures (cf. Rom. 5:14, Gal. 4:24), as did Saint Peter (cf. 1 Pet. 3:20-21). Saint Augustine summed up this interpretive method in a single phrase: The New Testament is concealed in the Old, and the Old is revealed in the New.

What unites the two Testaments is what unites God and mankind. In the Bible, this bond is called the "covenant." A covenant, in ancient cultures, was a solemn agreement that created a family relation. Marriage was a covenant, as was the adoption of a child. When a family welcomed a new member, both parties would seal the covenant by swearing a sacred oath, sharing a common meal, and offering a sacrifice. Periodically, the two parties might repeat the sacred oath, along with the meal and sacrifice, in order to renew the covenant bond. This is how God made His covenant with Moses, for example, a covenant that was renewed annually in the Passover seder meal.

Nor did this arrangement end with our redemption by Jesus Christ. Indeed, the one and only time Jesus mentioned the New Covenant was in the context of His last Passover meal, as He culminated the sacrifice of His life. The only time He mentioned the New Covenant was when He offered His body and blood at the first Eucharist (Lk. 22:20). Moreover, Jesus commanded His apostles to renew the covenant with God by the same means. "Do this," He said, "in remembrance of me" (1 Cor. 11:25).

From the earliest times, Christians commonly called this action by the Latin word *sacramentum*. We find that word not only in the works of churchmen such as Tertullian (207 A.D.), but also in the documents of pagan officials who were investigating and persecuting the Church. Around 112, a Roman governor named Pliny the Younger used the word to describe the ritual worship of the Christians.

And what does *sacramentum* mean in Latin? It means "oath." Pliny said that the Christians in His province of Bithynia met before dawn to sing hymns and bind themselves by oath to Christ, as they shared "an ordinary kind of food."

Thus, in the witness of the early Church—and in the practice of our parishes today—we see the Old Covenant oaths revealed and fulfilled in the New Covenant *sacramentum*. All history, guided by the Holy Spirit, has led you and me to these specific moments of sacramental grace.

That's why most Catholics love the sacraments. We experience them as beautiful and dramatic ceremonies marking life's most emotional moments: a wedding, the birth of a child, the throes of a serious illness. Even the sacraments we receive more often we can associate with peak experiences. We remember the catharsis of a good Confession. Or our eyes well up at the sense of antiquity we get from a Sunday Mass in our old home parish.

All those emotions and associations are good. If we love the sacraments for their ceremonial beauty—if we revere them for their ancient tradition—if we experience them intensely—we've begun to see what they are. But we've only begun, and we have much more yet to see. Indeed, there's much more God wants us to see, intends us to see, and all but commands us to see.

To see the sacraments as God wants us to see them, we need to see more than the externals, more than the rituals. It's not that we should ignore the externals; we must never do that, because it's by their "outward signs" that we know the rites as sacraments. Still, the outward signs do not come close to revealing the fullness of the inner realities. So we need to see the sacraments "inside," too, if we're to see them as they are.

For that, we need *in-sight*—just the sort of insight Tim Gray gives so generously on every page of this book.

At the heart of his study is a profound intuition: Every time you and I participate in the sacraments, we live out an encounter that God has planned from all eternity. We enter a drama that is far bigger than the momentary ritual—far bigger than our individual lives.

Throughout the book, the author shows us how that sacramental history unfolded. Using the interpretive key of *typology*, he uncovers the many Old Testament passages that foreshadowed the sacramental signs we know today.

No doubt, you will leave *Sacraments in Scripture*—as I did—empowered for a richer experience of the liturgy. But, as time goes on, you'll notice something more. After reading this book, your experience of the sacraments will, in turn, empower you for a richer reading of the Scriptures. For the liturgy, which includes the seven sacraments, is the context for which all the Scriptures were written. In those many centuries before the printing press was invented, God's people received His Word primarily during the liturgy—in the readings at Mass, and in the liturgical prayers themselves, which were saturated with scriptural quotations and allusions. The primary means of biblical teaching and interpretation in the early Church was the homily of the local bishop.

For a Catholic, there's a very real sense in which little has changed since the days of the Acts of the Apostles. The Church continues to meet daily for the breaking of the bread and the prayers. Every day, the Church requires readings from both the Old and the New Testaments. And today, just as almost 2,000 years ago, those readings are not arranged arbitrarily; they're arranged typologically, so that we can hear the New anticipated in the Old, and the Old fulfilled in the New. This is the way we come to see how covenants work, and how we come to know the New Covenant in the breaking of the bread.

Once we can see these matters clearly, we will see the sacraments—inside and out—as they have existed in God's fatherly plan for us from all eternity.

That plan continues in your life and mine. Salvation history hasn't ended. It continues, *through the sacraments and through the covenant*, in everything you do and pray, suffer and celebrate, at home, at work, at leisure, and at worship.

—SCOTT HAHN

PREFACE

The goal of this book is to impart a deeper understanding and appreciation of the meaning and mystery of the sacraments. This study assumes that those using it have already received a basic catechesis of the sacraments. My aim is to provide a continuing education on the sacraments from a biblical perspective.

The subject of the sacraments opens up a tremendous vista. As a result, this brief survey of the sacraments is by no means exhaustive. Rather, the objective is to give the reader a vision of the profound depth of the sacraments in light of Scripture and salvation history. In particular, while there are many aspects of the sacraments that could be examined, this study focuses on the biblical understanding of the sacramental signs. And since sacraments are sensible signs of invisible realities, a deeper understanding of the biblical references for these signs should provide a deeper understanding of the invisible realities and mystery of the sacraments. My hope is that this survey might provide material for continuing biblical reflection on the sacraments.

—TIM GRAY

CHAPTER 1
SACRAMENTS
IN SCRIPTURE

The meaning of the sacraments flows from Scripture like water flows from a spring. What happens when a river is cut off from its source? Cut off the sacraments from Scripture, and the understanding and appreciation of the sacraments dry up. Too often the sacraments are taught without any reference to their relationship with Scripture, and thus many Catholics do not have a solid understanding of what the sacraments mean. For example, most Catholics have witnessed a baptism. But few understand how the water used in Baptism relates to the Old and New Testaments. Without this understanding, the faithful are unable to open themselves up to the meaning and mysteries of the sacraments (cf. Catechism, no. 1095).

The sacraments effect grace by their very operation, which is the meaning of the Latin theological axiom, *ex opere operato*.[1] "Nevertheless, the fruits of the sacraments also depend on the disposition of the one who receives them" (Catechism, no. 1128). How can one be fully disposed to receive the grace of the sacraments if there is no understanding of what the sacrament signifies? Without an adequate biblical formation, one could view the

---

[1] *Ex opere operato* is a "term in sacramental theology meaning that sacraments are effective by means of the sacramental rite itself and not because of the worthiness of the minister or participant." Fr. Peter M.J. Stravinskas, ed., *Catholic Dictionary* (Huntington, IN: Our Sunday Visitor, 1993), 205.

sacraments simply as Church rituals that somehow give grace—an understanding that leads many outside the Church to view the Catholic teaching on the sacraments as primitive ritualism or even magic.

Before I explain how Scripture sheds a floodlight upon the significance of the sacraments, it will be helpful to give a brief review of what a sacrament is. A simple definition of a sacrament is that it is an outward sign that gives grace. As Saint Thomas Aquinas wrote, "Sacraments are visible signs of invisible things whereby man is made holy."[2]

A sacrament consists of two parts, matter and form. This philosophical terminology, taken up by Saint Thomas Aquinas from the Greek philosopher Aristotle, can seem a bit abstract to us, but is really quite simple. The matter relates to the physical elements of the sacrament, and the form to the words used. Both are essential. For example, Baptism consists of the matter, water, and the form, "I baptize you in the name of the Father, the Son, and Holy Spirit." Both the water and the Trinitarian formula are required for the Sacrament of Baptism. Every sacrament has an outward sign (matter) accompanied by the words (form). Saint Augustine noted how the physical element and the word are the basis of a sacrament: "The word comes to the element and a sacrament results."[3]

Sign Language

The meaning of a sacrament is tied up in the sign. To understand what the signs of the sacraments signify is the key to understanding the sacraments. What is a sign? Something that communicates something else. A natural sign is smoke. When we see smoke, we know that there

---

[2] *Summa Theologiae*, IIa IIae, q. 61, art. 4.
[3] Augustine, *On the Gospel of Saint John*, 80.3; cf. Catechism, no. 1228.

must be a fire. Dark clouds are a sign of a coming storm. Flocks of birds heading south are a sign that winter is coming. We see these natural signs and they communicate something to us.

It is the same with man-made signs. These signs point to something beyond themselves by convention—that is, by people investing these signs with meaning. Traffic signs are a good example of man-made signs. A red octagon standing on an eight-foot post signifies that we must stop. There is nothing about the color or shape of the sign that inherently means stop. The sign communicates to us that we should stop simply by convention; that is, the traffic laws invested the sign with a particular meaning: Red was chosen to get people's attention, with the octagon shape for those who are color-blind. When people drive up to an intersection, they see a red stop sign but think in their minds that it *means* stop. The visible sign leads them to think of an invisible meaning. One thing is seen, another understood. A sign has tremendous power to communicate a message that transcends the sign itself.

Like natural and man-made signs, sacramental signs also communicate a message, but they do much more than that. One of the most important characteristics of a sacramental sign is that it is *efficacious.* This means that the sign effects what it signifies. In contrast, take, for example, a sign that is not efficacious. The stop sign at an intersection symbolizes that cars should stop, but it does not have the power to effect their stopping. Someone in a hurry may decide to ignore the sign and drive through the intersection. For the stop sign to be efficacious, it would not only communicate that cars should stop, but also have the power to physically make that happen. That is what is so unique about the sacraments; they have the God-given power to actually effect what they signify.

God's Masterpieces

According to the Catechism, the Holy Spirit is the divine artisan of "God's masterpieces," which are the seven sacraments of the New Covenant (Catechism, no. 1091). What makes the sacraments the grand "masterpieces" of God's work is that God has endowed the signs of the sacraments so that they truly effect what they signify. More than just signifying faith, the sacraments cause God's grace to be made present. This is the defining characteristic of the sacraments in Catholic teaching.

It was common in scholastic language to refer to the signs given by God in both the New and Old Testaments as sacraments. For example, circumcision was a sacrament. It was a sign that expressed faith in the God of Israel. But scholastic theologians, such as Saint Thomas Aquinas, always distinguished between the sacraments of the Old Covenant from those of the New. The Old Testament sacraments were signs, but they were not efficacious. Martin Luther and other Protestant reformers denied this distinction between the Old and New Testament sacraments. Luther argued that "[i]t is wrong to hold that the sacraments of the New Law differ from those of the Old Law in point of their effective significance. Both have the same meaning."[4] For Luther, the signs of the New Covenant are no more effective in giving grace than those of the Old. John Calvin also rejected any notion that the sacraments of the New Covenant had any special efficacy:

> The scholastic dogma (to glance at it in passing), by which the difference between the sacraments of the old and the new dispensation is made so great, that the former did nothing but shadow forth the grace of

---

[4] Martin Luther, *Babylonian Captivity*, chap. 3, part 1, as quoted in E.L. Mascall, *The Recovery of Unity* (London: Longmans, Green and Co., 1958), 97, footnote 2.

God, while the latter also confer it, must be altogether exploded. . . . The same efficacy which ours possess they experienced in theirs—viz. that they were seals of the divine favour toward them in regard to the hope of eternal salvation.[5]

Calvin well represents the Protestant reformers' view in holding that the sacraments are simply signs of faith, signs that do not effect any grace or change in their recipients. The sacraments are celebrated in order to increase and express faith, but in his view they have no supernatural power or effect.

Sign or Sacrament?

In order to illustrate how the Old Testament signs differ from those of the New, let's look at the example of the Eucharist. At the Last Supper, Jesus inaugurated the New Covenant by saying: "This cup which is poured out for you is the new *covenant in my blood*" (Lk. 22:20). Jesus' words echo those of Moses, when the first covenant was made with Israel at Sinai: "Behold the *blood of the covenant* which the LORD has made with you in accordance with all these words" (Ex. 24:8). Many animals were sacrificed the day the Old Covenant was made. Moses took half of the blood and poured it upon the altar, and the other half he put in basins from which he threw blood upon the people as he declared, "Behold the *blood of the covenant*." Why did the blood signify a covenant? Because covenants create kinship. Covenants create familial bonds, thus marriage and adoption are covenants, because they take two parties who were not in a familial relationship and make them family. On a natural level, families are constituted by those who share

---

[5] John Calvin, *Institutes of Christian Religion*, bk. IV, chap. 14, no. 23, as quoted in E.L. Mascall, *The Recovery of Unity*, 97.

the same blood, so this sign of family becomes the symbol of a covenantal bond. By pouring half of the blood on the altar and half upon the people, Moses was saying in action that the people of Israel and God were now covenant-ed—they were now family. That is why the prophets compare Israel's infidelity to that of an adulterous wife: because Israel and God were bound by family ties through the covenant.

The animal blood poured out upon the stone altar at the base of Mount Sinai and thrown upon the people was a sign that they were now God's family. But this was simply a sign: The blood they shared symbolically was the blood of sheep and goats. The blood in the veins of the Israelites was no different after the covenant ceremony. Thus the Old Covenant had signs, but they were not efficacious. For the sign of the Old Covenant blood to be efficacious, it would not only signify a blood relation, but would actually effect it.

Indeed, this is precisely what the blood of the New Covenant effects. Jesus' words over the cup at the Last Supper transform the wine into blood. And when the apostles drank from that cup, they actually partook of the blood of the Son of God, Jesus. Thus the New Covenant Sacrament of the Eucharist not only signifies a family bond between God and His people, but actually effects it. Through the Eucharist we share in the body and blood of Christ, true God and true man. The Eucharist is a sign that we are family, and as an efficacious sign it actually makes us family. For this reason, Saint Peter can say that we have "become partakers of the divine nature" (2 Pet. 1:4). This is the source of the apostolic teaching that the Church is the Body of Christ. No wonder the early Christians called themselves brothers and sisters in Christ, because through Christ the Church is the Family of God.

Luther and Calvin fail to make the crucial distinction

between the blood of the Old and New Covenants, the distinction between the symbol of the Old and the efficacious power of the New. How can they claim that the New Testament sacraments are no different from those of the Old? Circumcision was a sign of belonging to the People of God, but Baptism actually makes us reborn as God's children (cf. Gal. 3:26-27). In the Old Testament there were many kinds of ritual washings but, in the New Covenant, Baptism not only signifies a cleansing, it also actually effects a washing away of sin. If the sacraments of the New are no more powerful than those of the Old, what difference did Jesus make?

"But as it is, Christ has obtained a ministry which is as much more excellent than the old as the covenant he mediates is better" (Heb. 8:6). The New Testament often contrasts the differences between the covenants. "For since the law has but a shadow of the good things to come instead of the true form of these realities" (Heb. 10:1), and again in Colossians, "These are only a shadow of what is to come; but the substance belongs to Christ" (Col. 2:17). It is clear that there is a tremendous difference between the Old and New Covenants, between the shadow and reality, sign and sacrament.

What makes the sacraments so powerful? Why are they always efficacious? The answer is Jesus Christ. The sacraments are instituted and empowered by Jesus.

> Celebrated worthily in faith, the sacraments confer the grace that they signify. They are *efficacious* because in them Christ himself is at work: it is he who baptizes, he who acts in his sacraments in order to communicate the grace that each sacrament signifies (Catechism, no. 1127, original emphasis).

God has established that when the proper matter of the

sacrament is present along with the words, then the sign is efficacious, which means that the sign is a sacrament.

Water from a Rock

In order to illustrate the nature and power of an efficacious sign, let's look at an example from Scripture. As Israel was sojourning in the wilderness, the shortage of water was sometimes acute. The first time Israel ran out of water, the Israelites vehemently blamed Moses and also questioned whether the Lord was with them (cf. Ex. 17:7). When the crisis reached the boiling point, the people were about to stone Moses, but God intervened. God told Moses to strike the rock at Horeb and, when he did, water flowed from the rock. Years later, the people once again ran out of water, and once again they rebelled (cf. Num. 20:2-5). Again God told Moses to take up his rod and go before the rock. But this time Moses was not to strike the rock, instead he was instructed to "tell the rock before their eyes to yield its water" (Num. 20:8).

The Lord's command to speak to the rock in Numbers 20 teaches us how a sacrament works. The rock had already been struck by Moses once, yielding salvation in a miraculous way for the Israelites. Now the rock did not need be struck again: Moses needed only speak the word, and the rock would once again flow with the life-saving water.

The rock had previously been struck by Moses at Meribah. The salvation wrought at Meribah was to be made present for the people through the matter of the rock and staff in conjunction with the words Moses was to speak. Thus the salvation of the past was made efficaciously present through sign and word. This is exactly how a sacrament works. A sacrament makes present the saving grace wrought by God in the past. For example, the Eucharist makes present the body and blood of Christ.

However, the Mass does not re-crucify Jesus. In Mass Jesus is not sacrificed another time. Rather, the once-and-for-all sacrifice of Jesus Christ on the Cross is made present through the words spoken over the elements of bread and wine by the priest (cf. Catechism, nos. 1366-67).

Past Event	Made Present
Rock struck in Exodus 17	Moses to speak to rock in Numbers 20
Water flows	Water flows

Past Event	Made Present
Jesus dies on the Cross	Mass
Water and blood flow	Body and blood present in Eucharist

Unfortunately, Moses did not follow the rubrics. He did not speak to the rock but struck it two times with his staff. God reprimanded Moses, saying:

> Because you did not believe in me, to sanctify me in the eyes of the people of Israel, therefore you shall not bring this assembly into the land which I have given them (Num. 20:12).

Moses' decision to strike the rock again, rather than simply speak to it, was a failure in faith. To trust that God Himself will act through the sign and word takes faith. To believe in the sacraments takes faith in God. Failure to trust the power of God's signs can keep one from the Promised Land.

The rock at Meribah differs from a sacrament in that its power was to be a one-time event, whereas the seven sacraments of the New Covenant have an abiding power. Both the miraculous flow of water from the rock and the grace that comes forth from the sacraments derive their efficacy from God. The minister of the sacrament, like Moses, is not the source of the sacraments' power, but simply their instrument and steward.

Ultimate Power Source

The Catechism makes it clear that the effectiveness of the sacraments is absolutely dependent upon Jesus Christ. "Sacraments are 'powers that come forth' from the Body of Christ, which is ever-living and life-giving" (Catechism, no. 1116). In describing the sacraments as "powers that come forth" from Christ, the Catechism is alluding to the story of Jesus' healing of the hemorrhaging woman in Luke 8:42-48. As Jesus was traveling with a large crowd, a woman who had a hemorrhage reached out and touched the fringe of His garment (v. 44). She was immediately healed. Jesus then said, "Some one touched me; for I perceive that power has gone forth from me" (v. 46).

Peter observed that many in the crowd must have touched Jesus, since the crowd pressed upon Him. But only one person reached out and touched Jesus in faith, and that allowed "power" to flow from Him. How many Catholics go to Mass or receive Confirmation and nothing changes in their life? They are like the crowd that was very close to Jesus, but did not reach out to Him in faith. That, the Catechism says, is how the sacraments work. Through the sacraments we encounter Jesus Himself, and if we come to Him in faith, then power will flow forth for us just as it did for the woman whose faith allowed her to be touched by grace. The sacraments are channels of God's powerful grace, but that grace will bear fruit in our lives according to how well we are disposed to receive Jesus in the sacraments with faith.

Christ-Centered Vision of Sacraments

The grace of the sacraments flows forth from the "paschal mystery of the Passion, Death and Resurrection of Christ" (SC 61). The victory of the Cross and Resurrection are made present to the People of God through the sacraments of the Church. The sacraments are the portals of grace, the means God has chosen to abide with His people. The sacraments not only come from Christ, but they also make the life of Christ present in our lives.

> The mysteries of Christ's life are the foundations of what he would henceforth dispense in the sacraments, through the ministers of his Church, for "what was visible in our Savior has passed over into his mysteries" (Catechism, no. 1115).

The Catechism is quoting Saint Leo the Great, a famous fifth-century pope. By Christ's "mysteries," Saint Leo literally means sacraments. The Greek-speaking Fathers of the Church called the sacraments "mysteries." Thus the life of Jesus is given in the sacraments.

Why? Saint John Eudes claimed that the goal of our lives is to continue the life of Christ. Thus the sacraments are the means to living the life of Christ. Saint John Eudes says:

> We must continue to accomplish in ourselves the stages of Jesus' life and his mysteries and often to beg him to perfect and realize them in us and in his whole Church. . . . For it is the plan of the Son of God to make us and the whole Church partake in his mysteries and to extend them to and continue them in us and in his whole Church (as quoted in Catechism, no. 521).

We are powerless to live the life of Christ without God's grace. That is why the Catechism teaches us about the sacraments and the liturgy (the channels of God's grace) before teaching us about the moral life. There is wisdom in the ordering of the four pillars of the Catechism. First comes the Creed (Pillar I), for we must start with faith in God. Then comes God's action in the sacraments and the liturgy (Pillar II), which enables us to live the life of Christ (Pillar III). Then we can pray as God's children (Pillar IV). Grace must come before action, the sacraments before morality.

It is important to maintain a Christ-centered approach to the sacraments. That means more than just realizing that the power of the sacraments is rooted in Christ. Rather, we must also see how "what was visible in our Savior" has passed over into His sacraments. Each sacrament is rooted in the life and death of Jesus. Baptism, for example, is rooted in the Cross. Thus Saint Paul says, "Do you not know that all of us who have been baptized into Christ Jesus were baptized into his death?" (Rom. 6:3). If we simply understand Baptism as a rebirth and cleansing apart from the death of Christ, we do not fully grasp its meaning. Every sacrament must be taught in relation to Jesus.

An example of how sacramental catechesis can tend to drift away from a focus on Jesus Christ is illustrated in the way Confirmation is frequently taught. I often ask my students, "What event in the New Testament does the Sacrament of Confirmation refer to?" Their answer is invariably "Pentecost." When I inform them that they are wrong, they are genuinely surprised. Confirmation does not find its primary reference in Pentecost. Rather, Confirmation relates, as all the sacraments do, first and foremost to the life of Jesus. So to what part of Jesus' life does Confirmation relate?

The Baptism of Jesus is the basis of Christian Confirmation. When Jesus was baptized by John, He was also anointed by the power of the Spirit. The dove that descends upon Jesus is His anointing in the Spirit. From then on, Saint Luke tells us that He goes forth in the power of the Spirit (cf. Lk. 4:1, 14, 18). In the first recorded baptismal homily, Peter refers to "how God anointed Jesus of

Nazareth with the Holy Spirit and with power" when He was baptized by John the Baptist (Acts 10:38). Luke shows us that at the beginning of Jesus' mission He is anointed with the power of the Holy Spirit. This is what is happening in Confirmation—we are sharing in the mission of Jesus. Just as priests, prophets, and kings were anointed, so too is Jesus—and so too are His disciples. We need to be anointed with the Spirit to live the mission and life of Jesus. That is what Confirmation is all about.

How is Pentecost relevant to Confirmation? Saint Luke tells us that Jesus begins His mission with an anointing of the Spirit. In his sequel to the Gospel (Acts of the Apostles), Saint Luke also tells us that the Church begins her mission with an anointing of the Spirit. Luke parallels the anointing of Jesus at the Jordan to the Church's anointing in the Upper Room. To really understand Pentecost, as in the case of Confirmation, we must see how it is an extension—a making present—of Jesus' anointing in the Spirit. All the sacraments, as the following chapters will highlight, are rooted in the person and mission of Jesus.

Context Is Everything

The *General Directory for Catechesis* teaches that catechesis "should situate the sacraments within the history of salvation" (GDC 108). When the sacraments are taught, they must be explained in the context of salvation history, which means Scripture. This was the point of the discussion above about Confirmation. To teach Confirmation apart from Jesus' anointing or the Church's anointing at Pentecost is to lose sight of its meaning. This is why the Catechism, at the outset of each of its articles on the sacraments, has a section that places that sacrament in the context of salvation history. For example, the first section in the article on the Anointing of the Sick is entitled, "Its Foundations in the Economy of Salvation." By economy of salvation, the Catechism means salvation history. "Economy" is a biblical term, and in Greek it refers broadly to a family plan or household management. Saint Paul and the Fathers of the Church refer to salvation history as God's household plan—the plan for how God fathers His people through time.

The signs of the sacraments take their primary meaning from the events of salvation history: those events that were prefigured in the Old Testament and made present in Christ. Thus both the Old and New Testaments are very important in understanding the sacraments. The mystery of Jesus' anointing is manifest in the New Testament, but prefigured in the Old by the anointing of priests, prophets, and kings. Both shed light on the present meaning of the sacrament.

In order to understand the sign of Confirmation, which is the anointing with oil, one must know how the sign is related to the anointings described in Scripture. "Catechesis helps to make the passage from sign to mystery" (GDC 108), thus when one is anointed with oil in Confirmation, the sign leads them to contemplate the anointing of those chosen by God, most especially His Son. Reading the sign language of the sacraments is crucial to being Catholic. Thus Vatican II teaches: "It is, therefore, of the greatest importance that the faithful should easily understand the sacramental signs, and should eagerly frequent those sacraments which were instituted to nourish the Christian life" (SC 59).

Since "it is from the Scriptures that the . . . signs derive their meaning" (Catechism, no. 1100), it is necessary that the biblical basis of the sacramental signs be taught. This is why this book focuses on placing the sacraments in the context of salvation history. The approach taken here is not an exhaustive study of the sacraments, but rather a first step toward a biblical literacy of the sacramental signs. We simply cannot understand the sacramental signs without Scripture. The Catechism underscores how proper sacramental catechesis must enable people to read the "sign language" of the sacraments:

> Liturgical catechesis aims to initiate people into the mystery of Christ (It is "mystagogy.") by proceeding from the visible to the invisible, from the sign to the thing signified, from the "sacraments" to the "mysteries" (Catechism, no. 1075).

When we are unable to read the signs of the sacraments, there will be no movement from the visible to the invisible, from the sign to the thing signified, from the sacrament to Christ. That is because we need the perspective of the history of salvation to clearly understand the nature of the sacraments.[6]

The Book's Blueprint

Therefore, the method of this book is to place each sacrament in the context of salvation history. The chapters on each sacrament have three main parts. The first part places the sacrament in the context of the Old Testament, because "[i]n the sacramental economy the Holy Spirit fulfills what was prefigured in *the Old Covenant*" (Catechism, no. 1093, original emphasis). As Cardinal Danielou once observed, "[w]e rediscover the true symbolism of the

---

[6] Jean Danielou, "The Sacraments and the History of Salvation," as found in his larger work, *The Liturgy and the Word of God* (Collegeville, MN: Liturgical Press, 1959), 31.

rite by referring to the realities of the Old Testament."[7]

For example, the water of Baptism relates to the waters of the flood and the Red Sea. Water in Baptism is not merely a natural sign of cleansing, but also a sign of death, harkening back to the flood. Thus Lactantius (cf. 245-323) wrote, "Water is the figure of death."[8]

The second and central part looks at the sacrament in light of Jesus' life and death. "By this re-reading in the Spirit of Truth, starting from Christ, the figures are unveiled" (Catechism, no. 1094). The Catechism teaches that we should be able to see the relationship between the Old and New Testaments, as Cardinal Danielou remarked:

> Knowledge of these correspondences [between the Old and New] is the Christian wisdom as the Fathers understood it, the spiritual understanding of Scripture. And this is where the liturgy is the mistress of exegesis.[9]

The third part employs Scripture as a lens to see how the mystery of the sacrament is made present in the here and now of our daily lives. This "Application" section tries to drive home an all-important aspect of the sacraments. The sacraments make present God's saving deeds of the past. "Christian liturgy [including the sacraments] not only recalls the events that saved us but actualizes them, makes them present" (Catechism, no. 1104). The Holy Spirit enables the past victories of God to be made available to us *today*. "By his [the Holy Spirit's] transforming power, he makes the mystery of Christ present here and now" (Catechism, no. 1092).

---

[7] *Ibid.*, 32.
[8] *Divine Institutes*, bk. II, chap. 10.
[9] Danielou, *The Liturgy and the Word of God*, 23.

Past Made Present

When we read the Bible, we easily notice all the great miracles and mighty deeds of the past, and wonder why God does not act in our lives. But that is where the sacraments and the liturgy come in. Christianity is not a "religion of the book," in that we only read about what God did in the past; no, through the sacraments and liturgy God continues to make present His saving grace.

Thus the sacraments turn past history into present mystery. For example, God's salvation of Israel from her bondage to Egypt through the waters of the Red Sea and the anointing of Jesus by the Holy Spirit in the Jordan become present for us in the Sacrament of Baptism. In Scripture we hear what God has done for His people before us, but through the sacraments we experience how these deeds are effective *for us.* The liturgy and sacraments are our doorway into the story of salvation. Thus the covenant drama is not simply the story of Israel, Jesus, the disciples, and others, but through our participation in the sacraments, beginning with Baptism, it is our own story.

This calls for a Catholic worldview, a new vision to see how the sacraments make present the power and life of Christ in our lives. "The catechetical message helps the Christian to locate himself in history and to insert himself into it, by showing that Christ is the ultimate meaning of this history" (GDC 98). We see, then, that salvation history does not end with the death of the apostles, but continues in our day. Our lives are part of the story—our own story is a chapter in the life of Christ through all time. This is the mystery of the economy of salvation, that Jesus is prefigured in the Old Testament, made manifest in the New Testament, and "post-figured" by us living the life of Christ today. This is a profoundly spiritual vision that the sacraments invite us to live out. "But this also demands that catechesis help the faithful to open themselves to this spiritual understanding of the economy of salvation as the Church's liturgy reveals it and enable us to live it" (Catechism, no. 1095).

CHAPTER 2
SACRAMENT OF BAPTISM

Overview

The Sacrament of Baptism is the foundation of the sacramental life of all Christians. It is so important in God's plan of salvation that He designed many events to prefigure it throughout the Old Testament. From Noah's flood to Israel's crossing of the Red Sea, salvation through water has been a recurring theme in salvation history. This sign of salvation reaches its climax in the Old Testament when Joshua leads Israel across the waters of the Jordan, dry-shod, and then into the Promised Land. The experience of Israel is repeated in the life of Jesus, in yet a greater way, when Jesus comes to the Jordan River to be baptized with water and the Holy Spirit. Jesus is the new Joshua (Joshua is the Hebrew form of the name Jesus) who leads His people to the ultimate promised land, heaven.

Baptism in the Old Testament

At the very beginning of creation, "the Spirit of God was moving over the face of the waters" (Gen. 1:2). The Spirit overshadows the waters that will be the source of life (cf. Catechism, no. 1218). The waters are soon parted to allow for the land, a scene which will tragically be reversed when God withdraws His blessing in the time of the great flood. Water as a symbol is like a two-edged sword: on the one hand it is life-giving and fruitful; on the other hand, it is a destructive force that can drown out all life.

In the time of Noah, God sends a flood to wash away

all sinners. Noah and his family, eight persons in all, are spared during the flood through the ark that God commanded Noah to build. The flood waters cover the land, thereby reversing God's act of creation when He had separated the waters from the land. Sin had undone God's good creation. The waters in turn wash away all those who had sinned and abandoned God. After the flood, God re-creates as the waters recede, and the land once again reappears (cf. Gen. 8:1-12). God then restores His blessing upon creation and man, and a new beginning is made (cf. Gen. 9:1).

"The Church has seen in Noah's ark a prefiguring of salvation by Baptism," (Catechism, no. 1219). Saint Peter describes this prefiguring in 1 Peter 3:20, and then explains in the following verse:

> Baptism, which corresponds to this, now saves you, not as a removal of dirt from the body but as an appeal to God for a clear conscience, through the resurrection of Jesus Christ (1 Pet. 3:21).

Saint Peter sees that just as wickedness was wiped out in the flood, so is sin washed away in Baptism. The water of the flood destroyed sinners and yet saved Noah's family.

"But above all, the crossing of the Red Sea, literally the liberation of Israel from the slavery of Egypt, announces the liberation wrought by Baptism" (Catechism, no. 1221). As Israel made her exodus out of Egypt, the armies of Pharaoh pursued her. Trapped at the Red Sea, Moses stretched out his hand over the sea and the Lord drove the sea back, and "the waters were divided" (Ex. 14:21). Just as with creation and Noah, the waters part and the land appears; God's people are saved.

When Pharaoh's army follows after Israel, the waters return and wipe them out. The water that washes away the army of Egypt, which had enslaved Israel, represents the waters of Baptism that wash away the sin that enslaves God's people. Thus, following the teaching of the Church Fathers on Saint Paul's text in 1 Corinthians 10:1-4, the crossing of the Red Sea represents Baptism. This means that we make our own exodus through the waters of Baptism, and like the Israelites who were freed from the bondage of Pharaoh and his army, we are freed from the bondage of Satan and sin. The waters of the Red Sea have a twofold effect: They wash away Pharaoh's army and they part to save the Israelites. The water brings both death and life.

> Finally, Baptism is prefigured in the crossing of the Jordan River by which the People of God received the gift of the land promised to Abraham's descendants, an image of eternal life (Catechism, no. 1222).

Just as Moses leads the people across the Red Sea, so too Joshua leads them through the Jordan River. The waters of the Jordan part, and the Israelites cross the Jordan on a dry river bed, just as they had crossed through the Red Sea dry-shod. In the account of the crossing of the Jordan (see Joshua 4), the term repeatedly used to describe Israel's crossing is "pass over." When Israel passes over the Jordan and into the Promised Land, the Exodus is complete. Right after the Israelites cross over the Jordan, they enter the plains of Jericho and prepare for battle. Once again, just as the Egyptians were defeated at the Red Sea, so too the Canaanites who dwell in Jericho will be wiped out shortly after Israel crosses the Jordan.

Baptism in the New Testament

As Jesus is baptized in the waters of the Jordan by John the Baptist, the Holy Spirit rests upon Him. Just as the

Spirit of God hovered over the waters at the outset of creation, so too God's spirit now hovers over the waters of the Jordan and anoints Jesus, thereby ushering in the start of the new creation in Christ (cf. Catechism, no. 1224). Thus Saint Paul can say, "Therefore, if any one is in Christ, he is a new creation; the old has passed away, behold, the new has come" (2 Cor. 5:17).

Saint Mark tells us that the heavens are torn open when Jesus comes up from the waters of the Jordan and the Spirit comes down upon Him (Mk. 1:10). The word that Mark uses to describe the heavens being opened is *schidzo*, which is the Greek word from which we get the term "schism." The word literally means to "tear asunder," a strong verb that points to the fact that heaven is dramatically opened up and the Spirit set loose at Jesus' Baptism.

This word is found in only one other place in the Gospel of Mark. At the end of the Gospel, at the Crucifixion, as Jesus utters a loud cry and breaths His last, the curtain of the Temple is torn (*schidzo*) from top to bottom (cf. Mk. 15:37-38). The Temple curtain was in the inner sanctum; it blocked off entry into the Holy of Holies where the Spirit of God dwelt in the Temple. It is unlikely that the parallel between the heavens and the Temple curtain being torn open is a coincidence. Why has Mark juxtaposed the opening scene of Jesus' Baptism with the closing scene of the Crucifixion, linking them together by the tearing of the heavens and the Temple curtain?

Mark is highlighting the intimate mystery of the connection between Jesus' Baptism and Crucifixion. Baptism is inherently connected to the Cross of Christ. This is made evident in Jesus' words to the sons of Zebedee on the way to Jerusalem. The sons of Zebedee, James and John, ask Jesus if they can sit at His right and left hand. They are thinking in earthly terms, that

Jesus is the son of David and that when He comes to the capital, Jerusalem, He will begin His reign. The irony is that Jesus will be enthroned on the Cross, and those on His left and right will also be hanging on crosses. Jesus tells them they do not know what they are asking for! He then speaks of His upcoming suffering and death as a Baptism: "Are you able to drink the cup that I drink, or to be baptized with the baptism with which I am baptized?" (Mk. 10:38). Jesus understood there to be a profound relationship between the Cross and Baptism.

The Catechism notes that Christian Baptism finds its origin and source in the Cross:

> In his Passover Christ opened to all men the fountain of Baptism. He had already spoken of his Passion, which he was about to suffer in Jerusalem, as a "Baptism" with which he had to be baptized. The blood and water that flowed from the pierced side of the crucified Jesus are types of Baptism and the Eucharist, the sacraments of new life (no. 1225).

The Cross is the key to understanding the meaning of Baptism. Saint Paul explains that Baptism is an incorporation into the death of Christ: "Do you not know that all of us who have been baptized into Christ Jesus were baptized into his death?" (Rom. 6:3). How does Baptism signify our incorporation into Jesus' death on the Cross? By the fact that immersion signifies death, just as the immersion in the flood in the time of Noah or the immersion of Pharaoh's army in the Red Sea; both are types of the death that water can bring. Baptism then, is a sign of death, and of Jesus' death in particular (cf. Catechism, no. 1220). Thus Saint Paul explains:

> We were buried therefore with him by baptism into death, so that as Christ was raised from the dead by the

glory of the Father, we too might walk in newness of life (Rom. 6:4).

This is what Jesus had in mind when He answered the sons of Zebedee. Although they were not crucified with Jesus, through Baptism they were to partake of His death on the Cross, "the baptism with which I am baptized, you will be baptized" (Mk. 10:39).

Application

The Sacrament of Baptism, according to Saint Paul, signifies our dying and rising with Christ (cf. Catechism, no. 1214). Saint Paul tells the Colossians that "you were buried with him in baptism, in which you were also raised with him through faith in the working of God, who raised him from the dead" (Col. 2:12). Saint Paul then exhorts the Colossians to live out the dying and rising with Christ, which they experienced in Baptism, in their daily lives, saying, "If with Christ you died . . . why do you live as if you still belonged to the world?" (Col. 2:20). He reminds them that they should have a supernatural outlook on life now that they have been baptized into Christ. He commands them to "[p]ut to death therefore what is earthly in you: immorality, impurity, passion, evil desire, and covetousness, which is idolatry" (Col. 3:5). Saint Paul reminds them that the works of the flesh are part of the old nature which they have put aside in their Baptism, when they died to sin. Now, because of Baptism, they "have put on the new nature, which is being renewed in knowledge after the image of its creator" (Col. 3:10).

The new nature gives a supernatural direction to our lives, thus Saint Paul says:

If then you have been raised with Christ, seek the things

that are above, where Christ is, seated at the right hand of God. Set your minds on things that are above, not on things that are on earth. For you have died, and your life is hid with Christ in God (Col. 3:1-3).

In Baptism we not only die to the old nature, but we put on the new nature, adorned with the graces of Christ and with the Holy Spirit, which empowers us to live as sons and daughters of God the Father, in imitation of the eternal Son, Jesus Christ.

The waters of Baptism signify a death. We die, or as Saint Paul says, we are buried with Christ. The Old Testament prefigurement of this aspect of Baptism is clearly the destructive force of water in the flood and the Red Sea. Baptism washes away our sins as the Red Sea washed away Pharaoh's army. From thenceforth we are to put to death the works of the flesh and all sin.

The waters of Baptism also signify new life. Just as the Spirit was present at the creation of the world and at Jesus' Baptism, so too at our Baptism the Holy Spirit comes upon us and we are given, as Saint Paul says, the "new nature" (Eph. 4:24; cf. Catechism, nos. 1262, 1265).

Questions

1. How do the flood waters at the time of Noah signify the reversal of creation?

many drowned new start

2. In what way is Jesus' Baptism the beginning of the new creation? (See Genesis 9:1-17 and Mark 1:1-14.)

Spirit hovers over to anoint Jesus

3. Give an example of how water can be both a positive and negative sign in the Old Testament.

flood – washed away sinners and also saved

4. What is the connection between Jesus' Baptism and Crucifixion in the Gospel of Mark?

5. Read Romans 6:1-11. What is the relationship, according to Saint Paul, between Baptism and the Cross?

6. How does Baptism signify our burial with Jesus?

7. Read Colossians 1:21-23; 2:12-14; 3:1-4. How should our lives be modeled on the twofold structure of Baptism, that is, on the death and Resurrection of Christ?

CHAPTER 3

SACRAMENT OF CONFIRMATION

Overview

The Sacrament of Confirmation strengthens and confirms the seal of the Holy Spirit given to us in Baptism. The sign of the sacrament is the anointing with the holy oil, called chrism. Anointing with oil held great significance in the Old Testament, including cleansing and healing, but most important was its use in signifying consecration (cf. Catechism, nos. 1293-94). In Israel, priests, prophets, and kings were consecrated for their holy office by the anointing with oil.

Jesus takes on the Old Testament office of priest, prophet, and king when He is anointed with the Holy Spirit at His Baptism. At the Jordan, with the outpouring of the Spirit, Jesus is manifested as "the Christ," which is a title that literally means "anointed one." In Confirmation, our baptismal anointing is confirmed and strengthened, and so we too are anointed like Jesus, and thus we are Christians— that is, "anointed ones"—anointed with the holy oil which signifies the Holy Spirit. Our lives should then bear witness to the power of the Holy Spirit with which Our Heavenly Father has anointed us.

Old Testament

Anointing with oil was the central rite of ordination to the priesthood in the Old Testament. Moses received the command from the Lord to anoint Aaron and his sons with oil:

> Then you shall bring Aaron and his sons to the door of
> the tent of meeting, . . . and you shall anoint him and
> consecrate him, that he may serve me as priest. You
> shall bring his sons also and put coats on them, and
> anoint them, as you anointed their father, that they may
> serve me as priests: and their anointing shall admit them
> to a perpetual priesthood throughout their generations
> (Ex. 40:12-15).

The consecration with oil, the anointing, imparted the
office and mission of priest. The holy oil was such an
important part of the priestly consecration that anointing
with oil typically evokes images of the priesthood. For
example, the psalmist can compare the precious unity
between brothers to the precious oil of Aaron's consecration: "It is like the precious oil upon the head, running
down upon the beard, upon the beard of Aaron, running
down on the collar of his robes!" (Ps. 133:2).

One of the roles of the prophets was the anointing of
the kings of Israel. The prophet Samuel consecrated Saul as
king of Israel by the anointing of oil:

> Then Samuel took a vial of oil and poured it on his
> [Saul's] head, and kissed him and said, "Has not the
> LORD anointed you to be prince over his people Israel?"
> (1 Sam. 10:1).

Samuel later anointed David as king and, with the anointing of oil, the Spirit of God came upon David: "Then
Samuel took the horn of oil, and anointed him in the midst
of his brothers; and the Spirit of the LORD came mighti-
ly upon David from that day forward" (1 Sam. 16:13).
Priests, prophets, and kings had an office of such magni-
tude and responsibility that they needed divine assistance,
which was signified and effected by the anointing with

oil. Anointing with oil imparted the Spirit of God to empower those commissioned to serve God in a special way. The Catechism points out that "in Israel those consecrated to God for a mission that he gave were anointed in his name" (no. 436).

Every king of Israel was anointed with oil at his inauguration. As a result, during the exile the title for the future king who would lead Israel out of exile and restore the kingdom became simply the "messiah," which in Hebrew literally means "anointed one." The prophets foretold that there would be someone whom the Lord would anoint with His Spirit, who would redeem Israel (cf. Is. 61:1). All anxiously awaited the coming of the Lord's anointed one.

New Testament

When was Jesus anointed, so that He could be called the Messiah, the Lord's anointed? According to Saint Peter, Jesus of Nazareth was anointed when He was baptized in the Jordan River, where "God anointed [Him] with the Holy Spirit and with power" (Acts 10:38). When Jesus came up from the Jordan waters "the Holy Spirit descended upon him in bodily form, as a dove" (Lk. 3:22). Just as David and the kings of Israel were anointed with oil, so too Jesus, a descendent of David, was anointed (with the Holy Spirit) at His Baptism in the Jordan. Jesus' anointing in the Spirit marked the beginning of His public ministry; from that point on, Jesus took on the role of priest, prophet, and king (cf. Catechism, nos. 436, 1286).

After Jesus' anointing at the Jordan, He can truly be called Christ, because He is now anointed. Right after Jesus is anointed, He is "led by the Spirit" into the wilderness (Lk. 4:1). From the wilderness He comes to Nazareth, where He takes the scroll of Isaiah and makes the words of the ancient prophecy His own, saying, "The Spirit of the Lord is upon me, because he has anointed me to preach good news to the poor" (Lk. 4:18). Because of the descent of the Holy Spirit upon Him at the Jordan, Jesus fulfills the words of Isaiah and can therefore claim that the Lord has anointed Him. Jesus is the Christ.

Jesus begins His ministry and messianic mission with an anointing by the Lord. In his Gospel Saint Luke highlights how Jesus' entire mission is marked by the Spirit. Luke makes this point by telling us that after Jesus' Baptism and anointing at the Jordan, He "returned in the power of the Spirit into Galilee" (Lk. 4:14). All that Jesus does, from His miraculous healings to dynamic teaching, He does in the power of the Spirit. Jesus' mission is carried out in the Spirit, which is made manifest with the Spirit's outpouring upon Jesus at the beginning of His public life.

When Luke wrote the sequel to his Gospel, the Acts of the Apostles, he carefully showed the parallel between the life of Jesus (which he recorded in his Gospel) and the life of the Church (which is the subject of Acts). Just as the mission of Jesus began with His anointing in the Spirit, so too does the mission of the Church start with the outpouring of the Spirit at Pentecost. The Church, the corporate body of Christ, relives at Pentecost the anointing of Jesus in the Spirit. At the Jordan River, the Spirit came upon Jesus in the form of a dove, and at Pentecost the Holy Spirit comes upon the disciples in the appearance of tongues of fire (Acts 2:3). Luke has shown how both Jesus and the Church begin their mission with an outpouring of the Holy Spirit. At Pentecost, the faith of the disciples is confirmed and strengthened by the power of the Holy Spirit, and they immediately leave the Upper Room in which they were hiding to spill out into the streets of Jerusalem and to the world to proclaim the Gospel.

Application

What is it that makes us "Christian"? Is it simply that we follow Jesus and try to imitate His example? Not exactly. Apart from God's grace, we do not have the ability to follow Jesus and imitate His ways. Only with the power of the Holy Spirit can we follow Jesus. What makes us "Christian" is the fact that we possess the anointing of the Holy Spirit, given to us in our Baptism and completed in the Sacrament of Confirmation, when we are anointed with oil by the bishop. We are "Christians" because we are literally "anointed ones." The Catechism sums this up well: "This anointing highlights the name 'Christian,' which means 'anointed' and derives from that of Christ himself whom God 'anointed with the Holy Spirit'" (no. 1289).

The full force of the anointing we receive in Confirmation can only be grasped in relation to the primary anointing accomplished by the Holy Spirit, that of Jesus Christ (cf. Catechism, no. 695). Every action of Jesus' life gave evidence of the fullness of this anointing. Our lives should also bear fruit that is worthy of those who have been anointed in the power of the Holy Spirit. Just as Jesus was "led by the Spirit" after His anointing, we too should be led by the Spirit, as Saint Paul says, "For all who are led by the Spirit of God are sons of God" (Rom. 8:14). In our Baptism and Confirmation, we are anointed in the Spirit, and thus we all participate, to a certain degree, in the priestly, prophetic, and kingly mission of Jesus (cf. Catechism, no. 783). Through Confirmation and its graces, we should be emboldened to bear witness to Jesus before all people, sharing our faith as an act of charity to others and as an act of love for God. We must act, for our anointing is a commissioning. This means that we have been given a mission by the Father, a mission in imitation of the Son by the power of the Spirit. The Catechism states this clearly:

> By Confirmation Christians, that is, those who are anointed, share more completely in the mission of Jesus Christ and the fullness of the Holy Spirit with which he is filled, so that their lives may give off "the aroma of Christ" (Catechism, no. 1294).

Questions

1. Read Exodus 40:12-15 and 1 Samuel 10:1. Who was anointed with oil in ancient Israel during the Old Covenant?

Aaron (Exodus) / *Saul*

2. Read 1 Samuel 16:13. What happens after Samuel anointed David with oil?

Left for Ramah

3. What do the Hebrew term "messiah" and the Greek term "christ" literally mean?

One who has been anointed
one Greek title for Jesus Savior

4. On what occasion is Jesus anointed with the Holy Spirit? (See Matthew 3:13-17.)

Baptism in the Jordan

5. What event in the life of Jesus does Pentecost parallel? (See Luke 3:21-22, 4:14-16.) Why?

descent of the HS

power of the spirit to teach

6. What makes us "Christians"? (See Catechism, no. 1289.)

followers of Christ

Baptism

7. One of the graces and obligations of Confirmation is that we give witness to our faith in Jesus and the Church. In what ways do you give witness to Christ? What more could you do to spread the faith?

Live the faith Communitus

CHAPTER 4

SACRAMENT
OF THE EUCHARIST

Overview

The Eucharist is "the source and summit of the Christian life" (LG 11; Catechism, no. 1324). In the Eucharist, the sacrifice of Jesus on the Cross is made present. The sacrifice of Jesus is the summit of salvation history. All the sacrifices of the Old Testament prefigured the sacrifice of Christ, which completes and surpasses all other sacrifices (Catechism, no. 614). These animal sacrifices, especially the Passover sacrifice of a lamb, foretold the ultimate sacrifice of Jesus, who is the Lamb of God. Jesus' sacrifice atones for our sin and establishes a communion in His blood between all the members of the Church and God.

Old Testament

When Isaac was carrying the wood for the sacrifice up Mount Moriah with his father, Abraham, he asked his father a simple but provocative question. "Behold, the fire and the wood; but where is the lamb for a burnt offering?" (Gen. 22:7). This question must have hit Abraham like a ton of bricks, for he was bringing his beloved son up Mount Moriah in order to sacrifice him as the Lord commanded. Abraham, the great father of faith, gave his son a prophetic, faith-filled answer: "God will provide himself the lamb for a burnt offering, my son" (Gen. 22:8). God does provide for Abraham and Isaac, and at the last minute Isaac is spared and a ram is found caught in the thicket. It is interesting to note, however, that it is a ram that is sacrificed and not a lamb: Abraham had foretold that God would provide a lamb—and that was yet to happen.

Indeed, this subtle but significant fact is recognized by the writer of Genesis, for the narrator comments on the name that Abraham gave the place where Isaac was offered: "So Abraham called the name of that place The Lord will provide; as it is said to this day, 'On the mount of the Lord it shall be provided'" (Gen. 22:14). Notice that Abraham said that the Lord "shall provide," and not "has provided." Abraham recognized that the ram was not the final sacrifice that God would offer. In the future, a lamb would be offered to atone for sin once and for all. Abraham and Israel would journey through salvation history in anticipation of the day when the Lord would provide the lamb, Himself.

The lamb became an important sacrifice for Israel in her exodus from Egyptian bondage. On the night of the Passover, the Israelites were commanded to take a male lamb without blemish and sacrifice it, and then eat its flesh (Ex. 12:1-13). Moses carefully laid out the prescriptions governing the sacrifice, such as the fact that no bone of the lamb was to be broken (Ex. 12:46). When the angel of the Lord came that night, he was to pass over the homes where he saw the blood of the Passover lamb. The blood of the lamb brought salvation. The Passover lamb, however, was not the lamb that Abraham had foretold. Rather, the Passover lamb prefigured the one final Lamb, Jesus. The blood of the Passover lamb was a sign of the true Lamb of God yet to come, Jesus (cf. Catechism, no. 1340).

Later, Isaiah prophesied to the exiled Israelites in Babylon that God would one day bring about a new exodus, one that would redeem Israel and restore her kingdom. Chapter 52 of Isaiah describes this new exodus, saying that it will be greater than the first exodus, for they will not need to make the new exodus in haste. After announcing the new exodus, Isaiah immediately describes the new Passover lamb of the new exodus, in what is now known as the fourth suffering servant song (Is. 52:13-53:12). In this song, Isaiah describes how the suffering servant will be "an offering for sin," who will "bear their iniquities" (Is. 53:10-11). This sounds like the lamb that Abraham said God would provide. Indeed, Isaiah describes the suffering servant as a Passover lamb:

> He was oppressed, and he was afflicted, yet he opened not his mouth; like a lamb that is led to the slaughter, and like a sheep that before his shearers is dumb, so he opened not his mouth (Is. 53:7).

The suffering servant is to be the long-awaited lamb.

New Testament

When John the Baptist saw Jesus coming to him, he cried out, "Behold, the Lamb of God, who takes away the sin of the world!" (Jn. 1:29). John's declaration about Jesus would make perfect sense to the Jews who had anticipated, with Abraham, that the Lord would provide a lamb and, with Isaiah, that this lamb would atone for the sins of the world. John the Baptist prophetically revealed:

> Jesus is at the same time the suffering Servant who silently allows himself to be led to the slaughter and who bears the sin of the multitudes, and also the Paschal Lamb, the symbol of Israel's redemption at the first Passover (Catechism, no. 608).

Saint John, the beloved disciple, describes the passion and death of Jesus in a way that highlights the fact that Jesus is the new Passover Lamb. John tells us that the hour when Jesus was nailed to the Cross was the sixth hour, the very hour that the Passover lambs were being sacrificed in the Temple: "Now it was the day of Preparation of the Passover; it was about the sixth hour" (Jn. 19:14). Jesus is the true Passover Lamb, sacrificed for all. This becomes clear in John's description of the Crucifixion. John writes that the soldiers came to break the legs of Jesus and those crucified with Him in order to hasten their deaths, since the Jews wanted them buried before sunset, which marked the beginning of the Sabbath. The soldiers, John recounts, break the legs of the two thieves crucified with Christ, but when they come to Jesus they find Him already dead. One of the soldiers, to ensure that Jesus is dead, thrusts his spear into Jesus' side, from which blood and water flow. John notes that the soldiers' failure to break Jesus' legs fulfills the scriptural law concerning the Passover lamb: "For these things took place that the scripture might be fulfilled, 'Not a bone of him shall be broken'" (Jn. 19:36). Moses prescribed that no bone of the Passover lamb could be broken, and so the soldiers do not break any bones of the true Passover Lamb, Jesus Christ.

Isaac's question, "Where is the lamb for the sacrifice?" is answered by John: The Lamb is on the Cross, and His name is Jesus. Isaac, the only beloved son, and Abraham, his loving father, had prefigured the ultimate sacrifice that was to take place on Calvary, when the heavenly Father allowed the sacrifice of His only beloved son, Jesus. It is not accidental that Calvary is part of the mountain range of Moriah, the very place that Abraham prophetically named, "The Lord shall provide." Jesus is the one whom Isaiah foretold would go to the slaughter with the meekness of a lamb.

The day of the Crucifixion was not the last time that John would see the sacrifice of the Lamb of God. According to the Book of Revelation, John saw the slain Lamb of God "on the Lord's day" (Rev. 1:10), which was a technical term for Sunday—the day Christians gathered to celebrate the Eucharist—which was the day of the week when Jesus rose from the dead. On that day, possibly during the liturgy, John is taken up in the Spirit to heaven. In one of his many visions, he sees "a Lamb standing, as though it had been slain" (Rev. 5:6), and then the twenty-four elders and the angels in heaven sing with a loud voice:

> Worthy are thou to take the scroll and to open its seals, for thou wast slain and by thy blood didst ransom men for God. . . . Worthy is the Lamb who was slain (Rev. 5:9, 12).

The Lamb appears slain, for in the heavenly liturgy the sacrifice of the lamb is perpetually present—just as the Lamb is present in the Eucharist at the earthly liturgy, which participates in and anticipates the heavenly liturgy. The blood of Jesus is the blood of the new exodus, an exodus that liberates us from sin. We are to worship the Lamb on earth as He is worshipped in heaven. So too in the Mass we are called to give praise and thanks to the Lamb, "Worthy is the Lamb who was slain!"

Application
Since Christ died for us, Saint Peter reminds Christians to live a life worthy of Him:

> You know that you were ransomed from the futile ways inherited from your fathers, not with perishable things such as silver or gold, but with the precious blood of Christ, like that of a lamb without blemish or spot (1 Pet. 1:18-19).

In antiquity, those who became slaves because of debt could be ransomed with gold and silver—that is, by the paying off of their debt. Saint Peter explains that Jesus has ransomed us from the debt of sin, not by money—but rather at a far higher price, the blood of Christ, the spotless Lamb of God. Thus Saint Paul can exclaim, "You are not your own; you were bought with a price. So glorify God in your body" (1 Cor. 6:19-20).

At the first Passover, it was not enough simply to sacrifice the lamb, the Israelites had to eat its flesh as well (Ex. 12:8). It is the same at the new Passover: Jesus commands us to eat the flesh of the new Passover Lamb—the Lamb of God. Since Jesus is the Lamb, we are to eat of His flesh, from His body that bled and died on the Cross. When Jesus taught this, many responded with incredulity, saying, "This is a hard saying; who can listen to it?" (Jn. 6:60).

In the Old Testament era, Israel was forbidden to drink the blood of animals, and yet Jesus said, "Truly, truly, I say to you, unless you eat the flesh of the Son of man and drink his blood, you have no life in you" (Jn. 6:53). It would seem that Jesus is contradicting the law of Leviticus which says, "You shall not eat the blood of any creature, for the life of every creature is its blood; whoever eats it shall be cut off" (Lev. 17:14). God outlawed Israel from drinking the blood of animals because that was their life force; God did not want Israel to participate in the life of the beasts. They could, however, eat of the flesh of certain animal sacrifices, for eating the flesh of animals signified a participation in their death; God did want Israel to die to the animal nature.

Why, then, does Jesus command us to eat His flesh and to drink His blood? Because God wants us to participate in the death *and* Resurrection of Jesus. When we drink the blood of Jesus we are not participating in the blood of creatures, but of the Creator; not the blood of beasts, but of the Lamb of God!

In the Eucharist we are called to share in the life of God. Jesus Himself taught:

> I am the living bread which came down from heaven; if any one eats of this bread, he will live for ever; and the bread which I shall give for the life of the world is my flesh (Jn. 6:51).

In the Eucharistic celebration, by the words of Christ and the invocation of the Holy Spirit, bread and wine become the very body and blood of Christ (Catechism, no. 1333). By consuming these gifts of Christ's flesh and blood, we share in God's eternal life. Through the Eucharist we become, as Saint Peter boldly says, "partakers of the divine nature" (2 Pet. 1:4).

We should receive Holy Communion with great reverence and love, for Saint Paul has warned us:

> Whoever, therefore, eats the bread or drinks the cup of the Lord in an unworthy manner will be guilty of profaning the body and blood of the Lord. Let a man examine himself, and so eat of the bread and drink of the cup (1 Cor. 11:27-28).

This is one reason why the Church has called us to make frequent use of the Sacrament of Reconciliation. Saint Paul speaks of the purging of sin, so that we can receive the Lamb with purity:

> Cleanse out the old leaven that you may be a new lump, as you really are unleavened. For Christ, our paschal lamb, has been sacrificed. Let us, therefore, celebrate the festival, not with the old leaven, the leaven of malice and

evil, but with the unleavened bread of sincerity and truth (1 Cor. 5:7-8).

According to the Book of Revelation, at the end of history there will be a great banquet in heaven, of which the Eucharist is just a foretaste. Those who have washed their robes in the blood of the Lamb will be invited (Rev. 7:14). When John is given a vision of this great heavenly banquet, an angel anounces: "Blessed are those who are invited to the marriage supper of the Lamb" (Rev. 19:9). We are invited to join the angels and saints in heaven in worshipping the Lamb of God who takes away the sins of the world.

Questions

1. What is the significance in the name that Abraham gives to the spot where he was going to sacrifice Isaac, "The LORD shall provide" (Gen. 22:14)?

Coming of a pure sacrifice

2. What is the role of the lamb during the Passover?

Sacrifice - to eat the flesh

3. Read Exodus 12:1-13, 43-46. What were some of the laws concerning the Passover lamb?

Pure male no blemish - sacrifice
Eat its flesh. No bone broken -

4. According to Isaiah, what is the role of the suffering servant in the new exodus? (See Isaiah 52:1-53:12.)

will be an offering for sins
who will bear their iniquities

5. How would John the Baptist's declaration that Jesus was the "Lamb of God" have been understood by the Jews of his day?

from OT - the Lord would provide
the Lamb

6. What is the biblical significance of eating Christ's flesh and drinking His blood in the Eucharist? (See John 6:51.)

I am the living bread that came
down from heaven - If anyone eats this bread
He will live forever

7. Read John 19:31-37. How does Saint John the Evangelist depict Jesus' Crucifixion so as to reveal Jesus as the new Passover Lamb?

No bones broken - blood + H₂O - pierced

8. According to the following verses, how should our daily lives reflect our participation in the Church's liturgy?

a. 1 Corinthians 5:7-8

Bread
get rid of the old and make
celebrate the new -
cleanse the temple of old - bread only
unleavened - pure and eaten for 7 days
keep sinners unbelievers out

b. 1 Corinthians 6:19-20

do you not know that your body is a temple of the H.S. within you — from God — God died for you — we are got at a great price —

c. 1 Corinthians 11:27-28 *Re Eucharist*

Who ever eats + drinks the cup of the lord unworthily drinks judgment on himself

d. Colossians 1:19-23, 3:12-14

In him the fulness of God was pleased to dwell & through him reconcile all to himself

Put on, as God's chosen — Holy and beloved compassion, kindness lowliness meekness

e. Revelation 5:6-14 *patience — forgiveness — meet — Lord —*

9. Read 1 Chronicles 16:1-37. In the Old Testament, the Levites were appointed to minister continually before the ark of the covenant giving thanks and praise to God. How might this Old Testament prefigurement encourage our own devotion to and participation in perpetual adoration of our Eucharistic Lord?

CHAPTER 5

SACRAMENT OF PENANCE AND RECONCILIATION

Overview

Sin is before all else an offense against God, a rupture of communion with Him (Catechism, no. 1440). Over and over again in the Scriptures, we see this truth repeated for us. Sin severs our relationship with God and with one another. Sin hardens our hearts, enslaves us, and leaves us isolated and cut off from what our hearts truly desire, God Himself. Jesus' whole ministry centered on the forgiveness of sins. His very name revealed Him as the one who would "save his people from their sins" (Mt. 1:21). Jesus' ministry of the forgiveness of sins, which He began during His time on earth, is continued even now through the Church. Through this ministry we can hear and respond to God's call to repent and return to Him with all our hearts.

Old Testament

In the opening chapters of the Book of Genesis, as a result of their sin, Adam and Eve are cast out of the Garden of Eden, no longer to walk with God as they once had in their original innocence. The original communion enjoyed between the first man and woman and God was broken and, as a result, Adam and Eve and their descendents wander the wilderness east of Eden. This story is sadly replayed throughout the Old Testament. Adam and Eve's own son would become a fugitive, cast far away from his family and hidden from the face and presence of God because of the sin he commits against his brother, Abel.

Again and again, God's desire is to reestablish the communion with His people that was lost with original sin, and the people's sinfulness repeatedly destroys the bridge that God would build. We see this not only in the lives of individuals, but also in the life of the nation of Israel as a whole. Thus, the same generation of Israelites who saw the glory of Yahweh's mighty deeds in Egypt and rejoiced at the crossing of the Red Sea are not allowed to enter the Promised Land because of their sinful worship of the golden calf. And even during their wandering in the wilderness, the Levites encamp directly around the tent of meeting, thus shielding the Israelites, in their sinfulness, from God's holy presence.

This story of exile from God as the consequence of sin is seen with particular clarity in the story of Israel's Babylonian captivity. Having entered into a covenant with God at Mount Sinai, Israel enters into the Promised Land. For a while, Israel is faithful to this covenant relationship, but eventually Israel, in her pride, commits idolatry and sins against God, breaking the covenant oath she had sworn. As a result, God allows Israel to be taken into exile as a punishment for her sins and her refusal to repent. The physical exile is to be a lesson for Israel. Being far from her homeland and Jerusalem is to be a sign of her deeper exile from God. The distance between Babylon and Zion is an indication of the distance that Israel had put between herself and Yahweh by her sins. The fact that Israel's sins lead to the Babylonian captivity and exile from the Promised Land illustrates the destructive nature of sin. Sin enslaves us and separates us from God.

The exile was the result of sin, and the return from exile would come about only through the forgiveness of sins, a fact that the prophets often foretold (e.g., Is. 40:1-3; Dan. 9). But Israel required not only freedom from exile but, more importantly, she needed freedom from the death sentence to which her sins have convicted her. When Israel broke her covenant oath, she brought upon herself the curses proclaimed by Moses in the last chapters of Deuteronomy. Many of these, such as sickness, enslavement, and captivity, Israel had already suffered as a result of her exile, but one curse, that of death, still loomed ominously over Israel.

Likewise, our sins harm or break our communion with God. They often bring immediate consequences that we suffer through. Left unforgiven, sin's ultimate consequence is death and permanent separation from God. Like Israel, we need God's gift of the forgiveness of sins to restore us from our exile and death sentence.

The Old Testament not only attests to the consequences of sin, but also addresses the very root of the problem of sin, that is, our willful disobedience against God. The Old Testament writers often referred to the problem as a "hardness of heart" (e.g., Ps. 95:8). In the story of the Exodus, not only does Pharaoh have a hard heart, but God's people also have hearts of stone—so much so that God writes His law on tablets of stone to make this point (cf. Jer. 31:33). Moses had called Israel to "circumcise their hearts," but the grace for such a complete conversion was to come only with the New Covenant. Jeremiah holds out this new heart as a sign of the New Covenant. The promise of the prophets is that Yahweh will replace the people's hearts of stone with new hearts so that they will fear the Lord and follow in His ways.

New Testament

With this Old Testament backdrop, it is easy to understand why salvation from sin is at the very heart of Jesus' mission. Indeed, as noted in this chapter's overview, the name "Jesus" literally means "Yahweh saves." The angel tells Saint Joseph that this is to be Jesus' name, "for he will save his people from their sins" (Mt. 1:21). The Gospels are filled with accounts of the freedom Jesus brings: He casts out demons, heals the sick, restores lepers to the community, and forgives sins. Much to the dismay of the Pharisees and other religious leaders, Jesus is often found feasting with sinners who have experienced God's forgiveness through Him.

No account is clearer regarding the effects of sin and the joy of repentance than that of Jesus' parable of the prodigal son. Having cut himself off from his loving father and squandered his inheritance on sinful living, the prodigal son finds himself alone, miserable, and humiliated. Aware of his guilt, he returns home with a repentant heart. The father's merciful welcome and unconditional familial reunion with his lost son is held out to us as evidence of the response that awaits us if we but repent and turn back to Our Heavenly Father.

Jesus makes it clear early on in His ministry that the forgiveness of sins was to continue here on earth even after His death. On one occasion while Jesus is teaching, a paralytic is brought before Him. With the scribes and the Pharisees looking on, Jesus announces to the paralytic that his sins are forgiven. The scribes consider Jesus' words as blasphemy, for who can forgive sins but God alone? Jesus responds:

> "For which is easier, to say, 'Your sins are forgiven,' or to say, 'Rise, and walk'? But that you may know that the Son of man has authority on earth to forgive sins"—he then said to the paralytic—"Rise, take up your bed and go home" (Mt. 9:5-6).

The healing of the paralytic is a sign that Jesus' word of forgiveness is true. Jesus' forgiving of the paralytic's sins, and subsequent healing, signify that Jesus has the authority to forgive sins. The fact that the paralytic can walk home is a symbol of the deeper freedom Jesus granted him by forgiving his sins.

Saint Matthew tells us that when the crowds saw this miracle, "they glorified God, who had given such authority to men" (Mt. 9:8). Notice that it is "men" in the plural. The crowds rejoice that God has given this authority to men. Jesus emphasizes this point by stating that the Father has given authority "on earth" for the forgiveness of sins. Indeed, in the very next chapter Jesus invests His authority upon the apostles (cf. Mt. 10:1).

The apostles share in Jesus' authority over illness, unclean spirits, and the forgiveness of sins. The name "apostle" means "one who is sent," and the apostles have authority in the name of the One who sends them. Jesus tells them, "Truly, I say to you, whatever you bind on earth shall be bound in heaven, and whatever you loose on earth shall be loosed in heaven" (Mt. 18:18). The binding and loosing is the power to forgive sins. Jesus also tells them, "He who hears you hears me, and he who rejects you rejects me, and he who rejects me rejects him who sent me" (Lk. 10:16). Just as the Father has sent the Son and invested His authority upon Him, so too Jesus sends the apostles with the same authority He received from the Father.

The fact that the apostles—and the bishops and priests today who participate in their apostolic ministry (cf. Catechism, no. 1536)—have the authority to forgive sins is explicitly asserted by Jesus after His Resurrection:

> "As the Father has sent me, even so I send you." And when he had said this, he breathed on them, and said to them, "Receive the Holy Spirit. If you forgive the sins of any, they are forgiven; if you retain the sins of any, they are retained" (Jn. 20:21-23).

Therefore, in the Sacrament of Reconciliation, when the priest declares our sins forgiven, it is really Jesus who is forgiving our sins: "He who hears you hears me."

Saint Paul describes how the apostles share in Jesus' ministry of reconciliation: "All this is from God, who through Christ reconciled us to himself and gave us the ministry of reconciliation" (2 Cor. 5:18). The "ministry of reconciliation" is passed on through the Church in the priesthood. Saint Paul describes how God works through the priest: "So we are ambassadors for Christ, God making his appeal through us. We beseech you on behalf of Christ, be reconciled to God" (2 Cor. 5:20). The priest ministers on "behalf of Christ."

Application

In God's mercy, He has given the Church the Sacrament of Reconciliation to restore us to union with Him and to heal us from sin. In our own lives, we, like Israel before us, can become enslaved to our sins and find ourselves exiled from God's presence. We become prodigal sons and daughters who have taken the wealth of our family inheritance and wasted it on sinful living. The good news of the Gospel is that Jesus Christ has brought release from sin for those who repent and return to God.

This call to conversion is at first a call to a change of heart (*metanoia*), and an interior conversion.

> Interior repentance is a radical reorientation of our whole life, a return, a conversion to God with all our heart, an end of sin, a turning away from evil, with repugnance toward the evil actions we have committed (Catechism, no. 1431).

Jesus Christ desires to replace our hard hearts with His very own Sacred Heart, so that like Jesus we may say, "not my will, but thine, be done" (Lk. 22:42). Sin calls us to flee from God and unite ourselves with evil. With the new hearts that Christ desires to give us, we will unite ourselves with Christ and flee from evil: "For a holy and disciplined spirit will flee from deceit, and will rise and depart from foolish thoughts, and will be ashamed at the approach of unrighteousness" (Wis. 1:5). This interior conversion, however, "urges expression in visible signs, gestures and works of penance" (Catechism, no. 1430). The call to do penance is a result of sin's residual effects on the sinner himself, and his relationship with God and others.

> Absolution takes away sin, but it does not remedy all the disorders sin has caused. Raised up from sin, the sinner must still recover his full spiritual health by doing something more to make amends for the sin (Catechism, no. 1459).

Thus, the paralytic "takes up his mat," the leper is called first to go to the Temple to "make the offering according to Moses," and the woman whose sins were forgiven wets His feet with her tears, wipes them with her hair, and anoints them with oil.

In Baptism, God gives us His Holy Spirit so that we can live our lives in imitation of Christ. When we sin, we fail to make use of the graces God gives us. Out of His love and desire for our communion with Him, God has also given us a "second plank" to catch us before we drown in sin's dominion. Through the Sacrament of Reconciliation, Jesus Christ Himself pardons our sins and restores to us the family inheritance we so heedlessly squandered.

Questions

1. In what ways does the Old Testament reinforce the understanding that sin separates us from God?

a. Genesis 3:1-8, 23-24

_____

_____

b. Genesis 4:8, 16

_____

_____

c. Numbers 14:21-24

_____

_____

d. Psalm 51:11

_____

_____

2. In what ways does Israel's physical captivity and exile to Babylon reflect her spiritual state?

_____

_____

3. Who is described as being "hard of heart" in the following verses?

a. Exodus 11:10

_____

_____

b. 2 Chronicles 36:11-14

_____

_____

c. Daniel 5:20-21

_____

_____

And how does "hardness of heart" result in sinfulness?

_____

_____

4. Why is the salvation from sin at the center of Jesus' mission?

_____

_____

5. Where in Scripture does Jesus pass on His authority to forgive sins?

_____

_____

6. Who is actually forgiving our sins in the Sacrament of Reconciliation (i.e., in whose name are sins forgiven)? Recall the prayer of absolution used during the sacrament, found in Catechism, no. 1449.

_____

_____

CHAPTER 6

SACRAMENT OF THE ANOINTING OF THE SICK

Overview

Since the Fall of mankind in the Garden of Eden, suffering from sin and illness has been a universal experience. Jesus Christ made the healing of people, body and soul, a major part of His messianic mission. Jesus both forgave the paralytic of his sins and restored his physical health. He cleansed the leper from his leprosy, thus restoring him to health and to life in the community and thus to worship of Yahweh at the Temple. Jesus' "work of healing and salvation" (Catechism, no. 1421) is continued in the Church through the sacraments, with the focus of healing taking place in the Sacrament of the Anointing of the Sick. Jesus' healings were a sign that through Him the effects of sin were being reversed. When the kingdom is completed, we shall return to the joy of Eden; suffering, illness, and death shall be no more.

Old Testament

The Old Testament recognizes a connection between sickness and sin. The Catechism makes this observation when it says: "It is the experience of Israel that illness is mysteriously linked to sin and evil" (Catechism, no. 1502). Why is there this mysterious connection between sickness and sin? The first reason is that sickness does not enter human experience until after the Fall. Sickness does not exist in the Garden of Eden. The second reason is that God's covenant with Israel promised health and prosperity for obedience to the covenant, and disease and affliction for disobedience:

> If you will diligently hearken to the voice of the LORD your God, and do that which is right in his eyes, and give heed to his commandments and keep all his statutes, I will put none of the diseases upon you which I put upon the Egyptians; for I am the LORD, your healer (Ex. 15:26).

Illness enters the human condition as a result of the first sin, but once the cat is out of the bag, so to speak, it affects both the righteous and the wicked. The righteous man of God, Job, experienced this in a particularly acute way. His friends tell him that his illness is the direct result of some serious sin that Job has committed. Job denies this, and in the end God vindicates him. Job illustrates that suffering and illness are not necessarily linked to individual sins, and that those who suffer must endure their trial with faith in the Lord. In the face of great suffering, Job confesses his faith that God will restore his health and life:

> For I know that my Redeemer lives, and at last he will stand upon the earth; and after my skin has been thus destroyed, then from my flesh I shall see God (Job 19:25).

Much later in time, Saint Paul will echo Job's act of faith in the midst of his suffering and imprisonment, saying, "For I know that through your prayers and the help of the Spirit of Jesus Christ this will turn out for my deliverance" (Phil. 1:19). Illness and suffering came into the world through sin, and even righteous men, like Job and Saint Paul, suffer, but they suffer in the hope of salvation in Jesus Christ.

In the Old Testament, healing from God often came by the hand of His prophets. Thus Naaman, the commander of the Syrian army and a leper, set out for Israel to receive healing from his illness. On arriving at the home of Elisha the prophet, he is instructed to wash seven times in the Jordan River. Upon coming out of the river, Naaman's flesh "was restored like the flesh of a little child, and he was clean" (2 Kings 5:14). When he returned to Elisha, Naaman aptly summarizes the ultimate goal of all healing, "Behold, I know that there is no God in all the earth but in Israel" (2 Kings 5:15).

Physical healing is intended to bring about spiritual renewal. It should be but an outward sign of the healing of our souls, thus bringing us into a deeper communion with God. Our bodies will eventually die and return to dust to await the bodily resurrection promised in Christ. Our souls, however, live forever; thus it is here in our spiritual lives that we must most desire healing. Elisha is but a type of Jesus Christ, *the* prophet who would come to bring the true healing of His people.

New Testament

It shouldn't come as a surprise that healing was a hallmark of Jesus' mission on earth. Long before the time of Christ, Isaiah had prophesied that the restoration of Israel would be marked by signs of healing:

> Then the eyes of the blind shall be opened, and the ears of the deaf unstopped; then shall the lame man leap like a hart, and the tongue of the dumb sing for joy (Is. 35:5-6).

In fact, when questioned by John's disciples on whether He was the one who was to come, Jesus responds by saying:

> Go and tell John what you have seen and heard: the blind
> receive their sight, the lame walk, lepers are cleansed, and
> the deaf hear, the dead are raised up, the poor have good
> news preached to them (Lk. 7:22).

It could not be clearer that Jesus Himself saw healing as
being central to His work on earth throughout His entire
public ministry. Saint Matthew recounts how, immediately after coming down from the sermon on the mount
at the beginning of His ministry, Jesus heals a leper, the
centurion's paralyzed servant, Peter's mother-in-law, and
many others well into the evening (Mt. 8:1-17).

The Gospels make it clear that Jesus' healings have a
twofold effect: the healing of physical illness and the forgiveness of sins. Just as in the Old Testament, there was a
connection between sickness and sin in Jesus' ministry in
the New Testament. While the Old Testament connection focused on the sin, the New Testament connection
focuses on healing and restoration from sin.

The very first healing that Saint Matthew recounts is
that of the leper. The leper comes and kneels before Jesus
saying, "Lord, if you will, you can make me clean" (Mt.
8:2). It is interesting that the leper's request is not to be
cured or healed, but rather to be made clean. Leprosy was
one of a host of items that caused one to be declared ritually unclean. Once a leper was declared "unclean," he was
exiled to the outskirts of the camp (cf. Lev. 13:46) and
cut off from the community and from liturgical worship
in the Temple. The leper's request, first and foremost,
is to be made ritually (spiritually) clean, not simply to
be healed. His desire is to return to worship God in the
Temple, not simply for his body to be cured from leprosy. Jesus, seeing the man's heartfelt request, responds, "I
will; be clean" (Mt. 8:3). The leper is immediately healed.

Jesus makes an additional request of the man: "[G]o, show yourself to the priest, and offer the gift that Moses commanded, for a proof to the people" (Mt. 8:4). Jesus heals the leper, but also calls on the man to witness to the ultimate goal of healing by going straight to the Temple, the dwelling place of God. Yes, the leper's body was healed, but the real reason for rejoicing was the restored communion with Yahweh.

While healing was a centerpiece of Jesus' mission, He did not come to abolish all suffering and evil here below. Saint Mark seems to allude to this when he states that Jesus healed "many" who were sick (i.e., rather than "all" who were sick). Even Saint John the Baptist, who had witnessed faithfully to the Messiah, suffers imprisonment and, in the end, is beheaded. Jesus, Himself the Son of God, suffers Crucifixion and death on the Cross. Simply doing away with suffering was obviously not the goal of Jesus' mission. Jesus' physical healings are outward signs of the inward spiritual healing from sin. Just as sickness can destroy the body, in a similar way, sin destroys the soul. Jesus' mission is to inaugurate the kingdom of heaven and restore the sons of Adam to new life in Christ. Jesus' healings were to show, in a physical way, the greater healing that is needed, that of healing the spiritual wounds caused by sin. Sickness, suffering, and sadness will pass away, not in this earthly life, but at the bodily resurrection in the New Jerusalem (cf. Rev. 21:3-4).

Jesus' healing ministry is handed on to His disciples. This is made clear in Saint Matthew's Gospel, when Jesus sends out His disciples with His authority to teach, preach, and heal. The apostles share in Jesus' authority over healing illness, casting out unclean spirits, and forgiving sins. The name "apostle" means "one who is sent," and the apostles have authority in the name of the One who sends them. Just as the Father has sent the Son and invested His authority upon Him, so too Jesus sends the apostles with the very authority He received from the Father.

Application

The miraculous signs of healing performed by Jesus are signs of the victory over sin and death that Jesus accomplishes on the Cross. Jesus' primary intention, however, was not simply to take away all illness and suffering on earth. The Catechism explains why:

> By freeing some individuals from the earthly evils of hunger, injustice, illness, and death, Jesus performed messianic signs. Nevertheless he did not come to abolish all evils here below, but to free men from the gravest slavery, sin, which thwarts them in their vocation as God's sons and causes all forms of human bondage (Catechism, no. 549).

Whether our physical health is restored or not, we have recourse to the grace of Christ which will give us the strength to bear our crosses. Thus the Lord said to Saint Paul when He refused to grant Paul a release from a particular physical affliction: "My grace is sufficient for you, for my power is made perfect in weakness" (2 Cor. 12:9). Thus Saint Paul learned that "when I am weak, then I am strong" (2 Cor. 12:10).

This is important to remember when considering the effects of the Sacrament of the Anointing of the Sick. Anyone who is seriously ill can receive this sacrament. Saint James describes how those who are sick should ask the elders, that is, the priests, to pray over them and anoint them with oil:

Is any among you sick? Let him call for the elders of the church, and let them pray over him, anointing him with oil in the name of the Lord; and the prayer of faith will save the sick man, and the Lord will raise him up; and if he has committed sins, he will be forgiven (Jas. 5:14-15).

The Sacrament of the Anointing of the Sick effects grace, which brings about physical and spiritual healing and strengthening. Sometimes, though, we are called by the Lord to share in His suffering in a greater way.

By his passion and death on the cross Christ has given a new meaning to suffering: it can henceforth configure us to him and unite us with his redemptive Passion (Catechism, no. 1505).

Questions

1. In the following passages, what is behind the Old Testament's connection between sin and sickness?

a. Genesis 3:16-19

_____

_____

b. Exodus 15:26

_____

_____

2. Read Sirach 2:4-5. According to the Old Testament, can the righteous suffer illness and disease?

_____

_____

3. How does the healing of Naaman in the Old Testament (cf. 2 Kings 5:1-14) and the leper in the New Testament (cf. Mt. 8:1-4), point to the true spiritual meaning of healing?

_____

_____

4. Read Matthew 8:1-17.

a. How is the Anointing of the Sick seen in Jesus' healings?

_____

_____

b. How does Jesus' Passion and Cross give new meaning to physical suffering?

_____

_____

CHAPTER 7

SACRAMENT
OF HOLY ORDERS

Overview

Throughout salvation history the People of God have always had priests to mediate between God and man. The priests offered sacrifices to atone for the people's sins and officiated over the liturgy. The priests of the Old Covenant offered sheep, goats, and bulls. In the New Covenant, Jesus, who is at the same time the high priest and the sacrifice, offers Himself on the Cross to the Father in heaven. By virtue of our Baptism, each Christian shares, to a certain degree, in Christ's priesthood. This priesthood of all believers is known as the common priesthood of the faithful (cf. Catechism, no. 1591). We offer the sacrifices of our lives to the Father in union with the sacrifice of Christ, which the priest presents to Our Heavenly Father at the Mass.

Out of this common priesthood of all believers, certain men are called to the ministerial priesthood, which was instituted by Christ and has been passed down from the apostles. These New Covenant priests, ordained by the laying on of hands, participate in the priesthood of Christ by offering to the Father in the Mass the sacrifice of Jesus on Calvary.

Old Testament

When we think of the priesthood in the Old Testament, we usually think of the Levites, particularly Aaron and his sons. But before the Levites were made priests by Moses, there was a different order of priests. Before the Exodus, the father of every family was a priest. Each patriarch, such as Noah, Abraham, and Jacob, took on priestly functions, including the offering of animal sacrifices to God. The rite of ordination was the passing on of the blessing through the laying on of hands. This rite of ordination was usually reserved for the first-born son. In the age of the patriarchs, fathers were priests, and normally first-born sons were ordained because they would eventually succeed their fathers as leaders of the family.

The question then arises: When did the priesthood of father/first-born son change into the priesthood of the tribe of Levi? While Moses was on Mount Sinai receiving the Ten Commandments, Israel turned aside from the Lord and worshipped the golden calf. When Moses came down the mountain and saw the apostasy of the people, he cried out for those who were faithful to the Lord to rally around him. The tribe of Levi gathered around Moses. The Levites were the only tribe that did not commit idolatry with the golden calf. For their faithfulness, Moses told them, "Today you have ordained yourselves for the service of the LORD" (Ex. 32:29). This service to which the Levites were ordained was the priestly service of the Lord's tabernacle and, later, of His Temple. Throughout the Book of Numbers, God reminded the people that the Levites, not the first-born, were now priests: "Behold, I have taken the Levites from among the people of Israel instead of every first-born that opens the womb among the people of Israel" (Num. 3:12). Because of the golden calf incident, the priesthood was transferred from the first-born sons to Aaron and the Levites.

One of the primary roles of the Levitical priesthood was the offering of animal sacrifices for the atonement of sins. But the blood of bulls and goats could not take away sin or make perfect those who offered them, so these animals were futilely offered up throughout the Old Covenant (cf. Heb. 10:1-11). But God had promised the high priest Joshua, according to the prophet Zechariah, that He would "remove the guilt of this land in a single day" (Zech. 3:9). That day would come when Jesus would carry the Cross up Calvary. "On that day there shall be a fountain opened for the house of David and the inhabitants of Jerusalem to cleanse them from sin and uncleanness" (Zech. 13:1). What will be the sign that the fountain has opened up? "[W]hen they look on him whom they have pierced" (Zech. 12:10). What is the fountain? It is the blood and water that flow from the side of Christ when He is pierced by the soldier's lance (Jn. 19:34-37). Jesus is the sacrifice that accomplished the atonement that the animal sacrifices of the Old Covenant priesthood had cried out for and prefigured.

New Testament

The Gospels emphatically point out that Jesus is a descendant of the line of David, from the tribe of Judah. This royal lineage is essential for Jesus' claim to be the king of Israel, the Messiah. But some Jews posed the following challenge: If you claim that Jesus is king because He is of the royal line of David, from the tribe of Judah, then how can you claim that Jesus is also a priest, especially the high priest, since priests must be from the tribe of Levi? Either Jesus is from the tribe of Levi or the tribe of Judah: Which is it? This question arises in the Letter to the Hebrews (Heb. 7:14). The text answers the question by citing Psalm 110, where the Lord says to the royal Messiah, "Thou art a priest for ever, after the order of Melchizedek" (Heb. 7:17). The Messiah is said to be a priest, not after the order of Aaron and the Levites, but according to the order of Melchizedek. Melchizedek is the priest-king of Salem who blesses Abraham and offers up bread and wine to God. Melchizedek is a priest during the age of the patriarchs, before Levi and his descendants are even born. Melchizedek is most likely a priest in the order of the first-born sons.

Jewish tradition and the early Church Fathers believed that Melchizedek ("king of righteousness") was the throne name of the first-born son of Noah: Shem. According to Shem's genealogy, he outlives Abraham, and this would explain the passing on of the blessing from Noah to Shem to Abraham. This may also explain why Saint Paul stresses that Jesus is the *first-born* of many brethren (Rom. 8:29). As God's eternal first-born son (first-born does not necessarily mean that there are subsequent siblings; an only child, for example, is still a "first-born"), Jesus is the eternal high priest of God. Whether or not Melchizedek is Shem, it is clear that the Messiah, according to Psalm 110, would be a priest—not a priest of the order of Levi, but of the order of Melchizedek.

The role of the priest is to offer sacrifices for the atonement of sin. Jesus does not offer up the blood of bulls and goats, but rather He offers His own body and blood on the Cross. The Letter to the Hebrews describes the contrast between the sacrifices of the Old Covenant priesthood with that of Jesus:

> And every priest stands daily at his service, offering repeatedly the same sacrifices, which can never take away sins. But when Christ had offered for all time a single sacrifice for sins, he sat down at the right hand of God. . . . For by a single offering he has perfected for all time those who are sanctified (Heb. 10:11-12, 14).

In the sacrifice of the Mass, the one perfect sacrifice of

Christ on the Cross is re-presented to the Father for the sanctification of the Church. Thus the Catechism can say, "Everything that the priesthood of the Old Covenant prefigured finds its fulfillment in Christ Jesus, the 'one mediator between God and men'" (no. 1544).

Application

It can be difficult to distinguish the priesthood of Jesus, the ministerial priesthood that He established with the apostles and which is passed on through the popes and bishops, and the common priesthood of all believers. How do they all relate? Saint Paul makes reference to all of these, and a careful reading of his letters will clarify their relationship.

In his Letter to the Colossians, Paul describes the purpose of Jesus' death:

> And you, who once were estranged and hostile in mind, doing evil deeds, he has now reconciled in his body of flesh by his death, in order to present [*parastaysai*] you holy and blameless and irreproachable before him (Col. 1:21-22).

Jesus dies in the flesh in order to present the faithful to the Father. The word for present, *parastaysai*, signifies a priestly sacrificial offering. Jesus dies to purify the faithful so that He can make them a blameless offering to the Father. Just a little further in that same letter, Saint Paul refers to his priestly offering. Saint Paul tells the Colossians that "I became a minister according to the divine office which was given to me for you, to make the word of God fully known" (Col. 1:25). Saint Paul then goes on to describe what the goal of his divine office is: "Him [Jesus] we proclaim, warning every man and teaching every man in all wisdom, that we may present [*para-*

staysomen] every man mature in Christ" (Col. 1:28). Saint Paul's goal is to offer up the faithful to Jesus. The word for Saint Paul's offering, *parastaysomen*, is the same word used to describe Jesus' priestly offering. Just as Jesus offers the faithful to the Father, Saint Paul and the ministerial priests are to offer the faithful ("mature in Christ") to Jesus. In addition, the ministerial priesthood also participates in a unique and profound way in the priesthood of Christ when, at the holy sacrifice of the Mass, they act *in persona Christi* and consecrate the bread and wine into the body and blood of Jesus (cf. Catechism, no. 1548).

What about the common priesthood of all believers; do they have a sacrifice to offer? Yes, Saint Paul describes their sacrifice in his Letter to the Romans. Employing the sacrificial term for offering that we have already seen (*parastaysai*), Saint Paul exhorts the faithful to make their presentation or offering to God: "I appeal to you therefore, brethren, by the mercies of God, to present [*parastaysai*] your bodies as a living sacrifice, holy and acceptable to God, which is your spiritual worship" (Rom. 12:1). The sacrifice to be offered by the common priesthood is themselves! All of us are called to offer our bodies and lives as a holy sacrifice to God! All the frustrations and toils of daily life, as well as all illness and pain, may be offered to the Father. There is no tension between the different priesthoods, they all participate in the one priesthood of Christ, but each in its own way. Thus the Catechism states:

> The ministerial or hierarchical priesthood of bishops and priests, and the common priesthood of all the faithful participate, "each in its own proper way, in the one priesthood of Christ." While being "ordered one to another," they differ essentially. In what sense? While the common priesthood of the faithful is exercised by the unfolding of baptismal grace—a life of faith, hope, and

charity, a life according to the Spirit—, the ministerial priesthood is at the service of the common priesthood (Catechism, no. 1547, quoting LG 10).

Thus at the Mass we have the opportunity to offer ourselves and all the sacrifices of the day or week. At the elevation, we should unite our sacrifices to the sacrifice of the priest on the altar. The priest in turn offers the sacrifice of Jesus and, as Saint Paul did, offers the congregation up to God. Jesus takes these sacrifices and offers them holy and blameless to the Father.

Questions

1. Who were the priests in ancient Israel before the Levites?

before the Exodus fathers of family — Patriarchs Noah Abraham Jacob

2. What was the major role of priests in the Old Testament?

Holy of Holy — Rituals Protect the ark Blessings & Sacrifices

3. How did the Levite tribe become the priestly tribe?

anointed by Moses — Ex — Ex 32:29 —

4. How can Jesus be both *king* (from the royal line of Judah) and a *priest* (which at the time of Jesus was open only to those from the tribe of Levi)?

5. Read Colossians 1:21-28 and Romans 12:1. According to Saint Paul, what does Jesus present to the Father? What are the ministerial and common priesthoods supposed to present, and to whom are they to present it?

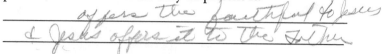

offers the faithful to Jesus & Jesus offers it to the Father

6. Do you understand the priestly role you have in virtue of your Baptism? How can you increase your appreciation and knowledge of your role in the common priesthood? How can you increase your appreciation and reverence for the role of the ministerial priesthood?

The common priesthood of all the faithful participate in each this every way through + in the priesthood of Jesus. Through Baptismal grace Faith Hope + Love. The ministerial priesthood is at the service of the common priesthood —

CHAPTER 8

SACRAMENT
OF MARRIAGE

Overview
At the very creation of man and woman, God instituted marriage:

> God who created man out of love also calls him to love—the fundamental and innate vocation of every human being. For man is created in the image and likeness of God who is himself love. Since God created him man and woman, their mutual love becomes an image of the absolute and unfailing love with which God loves man (Catechism, no. 1604).

The vocation to the Sacrament of Marriage is a call for men and women in their marital (and familial) relationship to imitate the kind of love which is characteristic of God—a love that is absolute, unfailing, sacrificial, and life-giving. Marital love is to be a godly love.

Old Testament
Since the nature of Trinitarian love is "absolute and unfailing," marital love is to be exclusive and permanent in order to truly embody the love of God. Because of this, we may often find it troublesome when we encounter many of the great figures of the Old Testament, such as some of the patriarchs or the kings of Israel, who repeatedly "transgress" what we know to be the truth of marital love. The Catechism teaches that in the Old Testament God allows certain practices because of man's "hardness of

heart"(Catechism, no. 1610). If we read the biblical narra-
tive carefully, however, we can see that even while allowing
such practices, God is teaching His people the truth of
marital love by the consequences that result when the fullness of His design is not lived out. The Bible subtly shows
that when marriage is not exclusive and permanent, it often
leads to bad results. So, for example, when Abraham took
Hagar as a concubine, she bore Ishmael, and the result was
a brotherly battle between the Israelites and the Ishmaelites
(modern-day Arabs) that continues to this day. When Lot
slept with his daughters, they bore Amon and Moab, from
whom the Ammonites and the Moabites descended, and
with whom the Israelites were constantly at war. When
Jacob took two wives and two concubines, he sowed the
seeds for family division, which was demonstrated when
Joseph was sold into slavery by his brethren and again later
when there was division among the twelve tribes. When
Solomon took many wives, he disobeyed the law for kings
given by Moses, which provides that the king "shall not
multiply wives for himself, lest his heart turn away" (Deut.
17:17). Solomon's heart did turn away from Yahweh (cf. 1
Kings 11:4) and, because of his divided heart, the kingdom
of Israel was divided in civil war during the reign of his son
Rehoboam (cf. 1 Kings 12). By showing us such disastrous
effects, these biblical narratives implicitly teach us God's
design for marriage at creation.

The true nature of marital love is most clearly demonstrated by Yahweh Himself in His covenant relationship
with Israel. The prophets spoke of Israel's covenant relationship with Yahweh as a marriage covenant. Yahweh
is described as Israel's husband: "For your Maker is your
husband" (Is. 54:5). In Ezekiel the Lord describes how His
covenant with Israel is a marriage covenant: "I plighted my
troth to you and entered into a covenant with you, says the

Lord GOD, and you became mine" (Ezek. 16:8).

> Seeing God's covenant with Israel in the image of exclu-
> sive and faithful married love, the prophets prepared
> the Chosen People's conscience for a deepened under-
> standing of the unity and indissolubility of marriage
> (Catechism, no. 1611).

Since Israel is covenanted to Yahweh, Israel's worship of
idols is considered marital infidelity, thus the Lord refers
to Israel as an "adulterous wife" (Ezek. 16:32). Through
Jeremiah, God describes how Israel broke the covenant
made at Sinai, "though I was their husband" (Jer. 31:32).
Yet, despite Israel's unfaithfulness, Yahweh is steadfast in
His covenant love and faithfulness.

Above all, it is through the prophet Hosea that God
illustrates the marital relationship that the covenant creates
between Himself and Israel. God tells Hosea to take a har-
lot named Gomer, for a wife. Gomer's infidelity to Hosea is
a sign of Israel's marital infidelity to Yahweh. The Lord says
to Hosea, "Go, take to yourself a wife of harlotry and have
children of harlotry, for the land commits great harlotry
by forsaking the LORD" (Hos. 1:2). The Lord then reveals
to Hosea that in the future He will make a new covenant
with Israel, a covenant that will mark a new and faithful
marriage relationship between God and His people.

> And I will betroth you to me for ever; I will betroth you
> to me in righteousness and in justice, in steadfast love,
> and in mercy. I will betroth you to me in faithfulness;
> and you shall know the LORD (Hos. 2:19-20).

The Lord tells Hosea that He shall woo Israel by taking
her out to the wilderness, where He shall "speak tenderly
to her" (Hos. 2:14). Just as Yahweh led Israel into the

wilderness in the Exodus and made a covenant with her at Sinai, so too, He will once again take Israel out into the wilderness before ratifying the New Covenant. It is not accidental, then, that the New Testament begins with Israel's going out to the wilderness to hear John the Baptist, who calls himself the "friend of the bridegroom" (Jn. 3:29).

New Testament

According to Saint John's Gospel, Jesus performed His first sign, which marked the beginning of His public ministry, while attending a wedding feast in Cana.

> The Church attaches great importance to Jesus' presence at the wedding at Cana. She sees in it the confirmation of the goodness of marriage and the proclamation that thenceforth marriage will be an efficacious sign of Christ's presence (Catechism, no. 1613).

Not only did Jesus perform a miraculous sign at the wedding when He changed the water into wine, His very presence at the feast was a sign of the nature of His mission and of the restoration and elevation of marriage that He was bringing about.

When Jesus is questioned by the Pharisees about Moses' allowance for divorce, He reminds them of God's original plan for marriage:

> Have you not read that he who made them from the beginning made them male and female, and said, "For this reason a man shall leave his father and mother and be joined to his wife, and the two shall become one"? So they are no longer two but one. What therefore God has joined together, let no man put asunder (Mt. 19:4-6).

According to Jesus, divorce and the breakdown of marriage is the result of sin: "For your hardness of heart

Moses allowed you to divorce your wives, but from the beginning it was not so" (Mt. 19:8). Jesus makes it clear that marriage is intended to be exclusive (monogamous) and permanent, and thus in His response to the Pharisees He restores to marriage its original dignity.

Jesus not only restores marriage to its original design, He elevates marriage to a sacrament. This means that marriage is not simply a sign, but a sign that effects grace. Jesus is the bridegroom and, through the New Covenant, He makes the Church His bride. Marriage between a man and a woman signifies the love of Christ and His bride the Church (cf. Catechism, no. 1617). As we saw above, the People of God were often unfaithful to the commitment of marriage, both individually and corporately. Indeed, this is reflected at the national level by Israel's covenant unfaithfulness to Yahweh. But in the New Covenant, Jesus bestows upon marriage sacramental graces that enable men and women to be faithful to their marriage vows. Likewise, in the New Covenant, the bride of Christ is given the graces to be faithful to her divine spouse. This is what Hosea had foretold when he spoke of how Yahweh would enter into a new covenant marked by fidelity and love.

Jesus often alluded to the fact that He is the bridegroom, and His bride is the Church. For example, when asked why the disciples of John the Baptist and the Pharisees fast, and His do not, He replied:

> Can the wedding guests fast while the bridegroom is with them? As long as they have the bridegroom with them, they cannot fast. The days will come, when the bridegroom is taken away from them, and then they will fast in that day (Mk. 2:19-20).

This may seem like a strange response to us, but it made sense to Jesus' Jewish contemporaries. In Jesus' day, the

Jews would celebrate a wedding feast for an entire week. The Pharisees had the custom of fasting twice a week, but they were exempt from fasting if they were attending a wedding celebration. Jesus refers to this custom to explain that His disciples are like the friends of a bridegroom during the wedding feast, and thus it is inappropriate for them to fast. However, Jesus does point out that a day will come when the bridegroom is taken away—a reference to His death—and then His disciples will fast.

Jesus often employed the imagery of a wedding feast in His teaching. Marriage was more than a metaphor to Jesus; often, it was a thinly veiled allusion to His kingdom. For example, Jesus says:

> The kingdom of heaven may be compared to a king who gave a marriage feast for his son, and sent his servants to call those who were invited to the marriage feast (Mt. 22:2-3).

The invitation to the feast signifies how Israel has been summoned to follow Jesus and enter into the kingdom of God. As it is in the parable, so it is in the ministry of Jesus: The invitation is rejected. Jesus uses this parable to show that God the Father has prepared a wedding feast for Him—the Son. This interpretation of the parable is confirmed by the Book of Revelation, where Saint John sees history climaxing in the wedding feast for Jesus and His bride the Church. The angel who shows Saint John the vision of the wedding exclaims, "Blessed are those who are invited to the marriage supper of the Lamb" (Rev. 19:9). Earlier, when Saint John recorded the events at the wedding feast of Cana in his Gospel, he made no mention of the names of the bride and bridegroom. Some of the Fathers of the Church believe this is intentional, to show that Jesus is the true bridegroom and the Church is His true bride.

Application

For those who have been called to the Sacrament of Marriage, the biblical accounts should renew our commitment to live out our marital vocation to the fullest. The covenant between spouses is integrated into God's covenant with man: "Authentic married love is caught up into divine love" (Catechism, no. 1639). The vocation of marriage should be a clarion call to each spouse to witness to the unconditional, steadfast, and everlasting love of our God. Each marriage should be an earthly icon of the love of Christ and the Church. Indeed, Saint Paul calls the Sacrament of Marriage a "great mystery" (Eph. 5:32), because it represents the spousal relationship between Jesus and His bride, the Church.

The love of Christ for the Church, and vice versa, is therefore a model for married couples. Saint Paul elaborates on this marital spirituality when he says, "Husbands, love your wives, as Christ loved the church and gave himself up for her" (Eph. 5:25). The way we love our spouse is to be a blueprint for how we should love Christ. Conversely, the ways in which we fail to love our spouse is often a sign of how we fail to love God. Marriage provides lessons in love that need to be contemplated so as to deepen our desire and ability to love God.

One of the great privileges and responsibilities of married love is openness to new life. God has blessed marriage from the beginning, saying, "Be fruitful and multiply" (Gen. 1:28). In this way, family fruitfulness gives witness to the life-giving power of love. Thus the Second Vatican Council and the Catechism observe:

> Hence, true married love and the whole structure of family life which results from it, without diminishment of the other ends of marriage, are directed to disposing the spouses to cooperate valiantly with the love of the

Creator and Savior, who through them will increase and enrich his family from day to day (Catechism, no. 1652; cf. GS 50).

Love is generous, and true love is modeled on the divine, which is self-giving.

The rich biblical teaching on marriage is not exclusively for those who are called to married life. All Christians, both individually and as members of the Church, are called to be as a bride to Christ our bridegroom. Indeed, the saints and doctors of the Church often describe the relationship between God and the soul, in the third and final stage of the interior life, as being spousal. Saints such as John of the Cross and Teresa of Avila refer to the soul as the bride of Christ. The Catechism refers to the spousal nature of the Christian life:

The entire Christian life bears the mark of the spousal love of Christ and the Church. Already Baptism, the entry into the People of God, is a nuptial mystery; it is so to speak the nuptial bath which precedes the wedding feast, the Eucharist (Catechism, no. 1617).

As we grow in the Christian life, the relationship between the soul and God is to be that of a marital covenant: steadfast, ever-lasting, sacrificial, and fruitful. Saint Paul reminds us of how we are called to be pure and loving brides to Jesus our bridegroom, when he says, "I feel a divine jealousy for you, for I betrothed you to Christ to present you as a pure bride to her one husband" (2 Cor. 11:2).

Questions

1. When did God create marriage? (See Genesis 2:23-25; Matthew 19:4-6.)

_____

_____

2. How are the effects of sins against marriage revealed in the lives of some of the Old Testament patriarchs and kings?

a. Genesis 19:36-38

_____

_____

b. 2 Samuel 11:1-5, 12:7-15

_____

_____

c. 1 Kings 11:1-13

_____

_____

3. How do the prophets characterize Israel's covenant relationship with Yahweh?

a. Isaiah 54:5

they spoke of Israel's covenant
relationship & Yahweh as a marriage
covenant

b. Ezekiel 16:8

Israel — the worship of idols like an
adulterous wife

4. How does Hosea, in his own life, embody Yahweh's covenant relationship with Israel? (See Hosea 1:2.)

forgives + is steadfast

5. Read Matthew 19:8. According to Jesus, why did Moses allow for divorce?

because of hardness of heart self love —

6. Read Ephesians 5:21-33. How is the relationship between spouses to imitate the relationship between Christ and the Church?

Covenant

7. How is marriage a sign of the spiritual life of the soul? (See Catechism, no. 1617.)

signifies the love of Jesus & his Church (Bride)

8. For each of the following properties of the marriage bond, how does authentic married love signify and bear witness to the love of God?

a. monogamy

no idols

b. indissolubility

oneness

c. fruitfulness

open to Children

_____

_____

FULFILLED IN CHRIST: THE SACRAMENTS
A Guide to Symbols and Types in the Bible and Tradition
FR. DEVIN ROZA

Using Scripture to deepen our knowledge of Tradition, Fr. Devin Roza's study of the sacraments sheds new light on God's plan of salvation—both in history and in the life of each individual. This comprehensive presentation of typology confirms, in the words of Pope Francis, that the Church is not merely a "human enterprise," but rather "a love story."

Organized by sacrament, Old and New Testament types and symbols are presented along with references to the *Catechism of the Catholic Church* and liturgical texts. *Fulfilled in Christ* is an indispensible reference tool designed for students, scholars, pastors, and catechists.

EMMAUS ROAD PUBLISHING

Call **(800) 398-5470** to order
or visit **EmmausRoad.org**

THE FULFILLMENT OF ALL DESIRE
A guidebook for the journey to God,
based on the wisdom of the Saints

RALPH MARTIN

This is a book to keep at your place of prayer for years to come. Drawing upon the teaching of seven Doctors of the Church, Ralph Martin presents an in-depth study of the journey to God. Careful reading and rereading will be a source of encouragement and direction for the pilgrim who desires to know, love, and serve our Lord. Whether you are beginning your spiritual journey or have been traveling the road for many years, you will find a treasure of wisdom in this modern classic on the spiritual life.

EMMAUS ROAD PUBLISHING

Call **(800) 398-5470** to order
or visit **EmmausRoad.org**

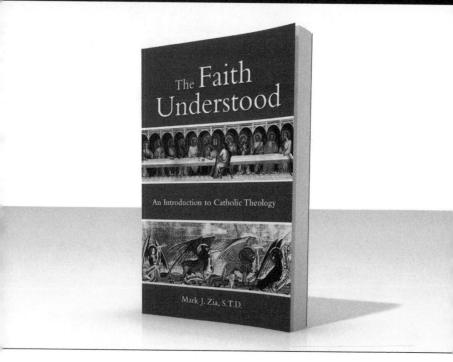